FOUR
POPLARS

Reverend Clifford Davies OBE

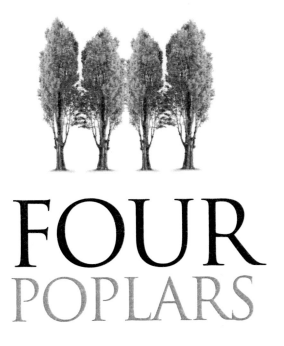

FOUR
POPLARS

Edited by Chris Newton

MEMOIRS

Cirencester

Published by Memoirs

MEMOIRS

Memoirs Books

25 Market Place, Cirencester, Gloucestershire, GL7 2NX
info@memoirsbooks.co.uk www.memoirsbooks.co.uk

ISBN 978-1-908223-22-7

Printed in England

CONTENTS

DEDICATION

Published in memory of our father and grandfather, Reverend Clifford Davies OBE AKC RN, on the occasion of the 60th birthday of our brother and uncle Jonathan Hugh Guy Davies and of his twin, our late sister and aunt Joanna Elizabeth Sayers née Davies.

Sarah, Stephen, Hilary, Penny, Tim, Georgina, Nick and Lucy

THE FOUR POPLARS

Foreword

I have had a feeling for a very long time that the memories of a happy and free boyhood such as the one I enjoyed before and during the period covered by the Great War should not go unrecorded. It is with this endeavour in mind that I offer this book about Wroxham in Norfolk, about the people who lived there when I was a boy, about the environment, both physical and spiritual, which surrounded me and which has had such an influence on the rest of my life.

I only beg of you to bear in mind that what I have written of the history of that unique community is what I have remembered from boyhood impressions. I have found that as I have sat down to write, more and more incidents have pressed through, as it were, from early recollections hardly heeded at the time they happened. I have not attempted to record events in a chronological order, although in a way that has seemed to happen, but rather to write about incidents concerning people and places and events, all of which have covered my life with influences too deep for words.

THE FOUR POPLARS

Preface

For some 38 years of my life, I have followed the profession of a parson in the Church of England. 26 of those years were spent as a chaplain in the Royal Navy. Having served a curacy in the parish of Bramford, a village just outside Ipswich in Suffolk, where I laboured for two years, a chance conversation with Cyril, a boy who was about to join the Royal Navy, set me wondering whether or not the service couldn't satisfy my somewhat thwarted desire to travel, and to travel widely.

When Cyril came round to say goodbye I told him that I envied him with all my heart this wonderful opportunity of seeing the world at somebody else's expense, and how I wished that such a chance could come my way. He, of course, thought that I was indulging in the old parson's glib talk of, "Well done, my boy etc" and, being a very bright lad countered with, "If you're so keen on going to sea, why don't you go?"

To which I replied, "How on earth do you expect me, at my age, a country parson, to go to sea?"

Quick as a flash, the boy said, "Well, I'm joining the Navy, why don't you, if you're so keen on it as all that?"

"How on earth do I do that?" said I. "I can't join the Navy at my age (I was then 30)," to which he retorted: "The Navy have chaplains, don't they? What about becoming a Naval chaplain?"

Now that was a thought which had never entered my head, and straight away I saw possibilities.

"That's a jolly good idea" I said. "I'll think it over". At once he jumped in, thinking that I was fobbing him off. "Never mind about thinking it over, write and find out what you have to do" he said. Turning to my bookcase just behind him, he picked out a copy of the Church of England Year Book. Rapidly ruffling the pages over (I told you he was a bright lad), he found the appropriate entries concerning the Naval Chaplaincy Service and informed me that enquiries should be directed to the Chaplain of the Fleet, at that time domiciled in the RN College, Greenwich.

"There you are," said Cyril. "Write a note asking for particulars and I'll post it on my way home."

"Hold on a minute" said I. "This needs a bit of thought. I can't go plunging in head first without weighing up some pros and cons."

"You're not committing yourself to anything, you're just asking for information" said Cyril. "Go on! If you really want to join the Navy, ask how to do it. You're only making an enquiry, after all."

He was right of course, so I sat down there and then to apply for the necessary particulars and Cyril posted the letter on his way home. By return of post came a letter inviting me to meet the Chaplain of the Fleet at Greenwich. I liked what I saw at Greenwich and the Chaplain seemed to like me. I had a medical while I was there and three months later, on September 30 1936 to be precise, I joined as a Chaplain Royal Navy at RN Barracks Chatham, a step which I have never regretted taking.

During the 26 years that followed, which included the war years, I travelled the world, met countless people, made wonderful friendships, laughed immoderately and enjoyed myself immensely. During those years I managed to retain my faith, my enthusiasm and, I like to think, my common sense; But above all, I kept my countryman's outlook on life. It is a simple philosophy, stemming from the fact of being born and bred in a quiet Norfolk village among hard-working, warm-hearted and contented folk, and it has stood me in good stead throughout my life and upheld me in many difficult situations. From time to time I have felt impelled to tell of some incident or other during my Naval service which to me has sprung, if I may put it this way, from deep-rooted passivities absorbed during my formative years. I will have more to say about 'passivities' in chapter 8.

Taking it by and large, a parson's life, in spite of all his manifold human contacts, can at times be a very lonely existence. This is all the more true in the life of a service parson, particularly if he is, as of course he ought to be, a dedicated man convinced of the truth and urgency of his message. More often than not he is driven back at times of stress to his own prayer life and disciplines proper to his high calling. Many such crises have I passed though in my roving life. Looking back now I can see more and more clearly that those things which have really influenced me in my life have been the values implanted in those early years, in my home village, by those 'spiritual pastors and masters' so despised in these loose days.

In moments of depression, fear, loneliness and sheer frustration, the pattern of living built up in me by those early influences during formative years - the eternal varieties which remain four square, in spite of the vagaries, temptations and wayward wanderings of the strange manner of life of the sea-faring man. I am minded here of Dr Johnson's famous dictum on the life of a sailor –

"No man will be a sailor who has contrivance enough to get himself in jail, for being in a ship is being in jail, with the chance of being drowned."

These things have been the gyro-compass of my life voyage. I have not always needed their counsels, but they have ever been there as the norm of true living, as the 'rock that is higher than I', the Christian's Standing Orders.

Many, many times have I sat in my cabin on board ship, revolving, like Sir Bedivere, my many memories. For many years I have toyed with the idea of putting those memories on paper, partly as an exercise in patience and perseverance for my own improvement and partly to fulfil a desire to share the happiness of my boyhood and its fruits with others.

Rough and tough we were, and our living in Wroxham, almost primitive during the first quarter of the 20th Century, but running throughout the whole of those marvellous years, was the golden thread of 'living for a purpose'. As I remark many times in the pages that follow, we were never bored, never without 'something to do', never without a purpose in our living. When I use the pronoun 'we' it is meant sincerely, for we, as a village, were aware of that modern theological catch-phrase, 'mutual interdependence'. We didn't call it that, in fact we didn't call it anything. Our elders and betters practised it, lived by it and we caught it from them.

It needed the jolt of a motoring hazard in the heart of my beloved Norfolk to finally spur me to put pen to paper and share my precious memories with others. I am more than grateful for the happiness that was mine. I have done no research, except in my own memories.

My story covers 12 important years of my early life in Wroxham, the years 1912 – 1924, from the age of six to my leaving home for the first time at the age of eighteen. I have tried to portray our manner of living. I have discussed our work and our play, the processes of our education both sacred and profane, (although for most of the time the one was the other and there was 'no difference or inequality', as the Athanasian Creed so aptly puts it), our simple pleasures, our happiness and our griefs

CHAPTER ONE

A unique village

"The past has revealed to me how the future is built"
Teilhard de Chardin, 1935

I have already called this book of memories Four Poplars and it would be as well, and for my own satisfaction, that I should give my reasons for the title. My early life in the village of Wroxham, some seven miles north of Norwich, was centred around four focal points. First of all there was the old schoolhouse attached to the village school, where my father was headmaster for more than 34 years. The schoolhouse was my home for the first 18 years of my life.

Secondly there was a field known as the Caen Meadow, between the schoolhouse and the river Bure, which wound its lazy way through our village. The meadow was the playground of my boyhood; more of it anon.

The next focal point was the village church, the Church of St Mary the Virgin, as it was described on the painted notice board in the porch. St Mary's was clearly visible from both schoolhouse and meadow. The church was almost my second home and it became a great and abiding influence upon me.

Finally there were the Four Poplars. These trees stood in the Caen Meadow opposite an indentation in the river bank which we called the Bay. It was the village swimming place. There I took my first plunge into the fresh waters of the Bure, and there I learned to swim.

In the high days of summer we became almost water-babies. I remember one summer day when Eric Stevenson, my boon companion, now a famous blacksmith and artist in wrought ironwork, and I spent all day down at the Bay with picnic meals. We were in and out of the water all day long, indeed well into late evening. Our parents were out at some function or other and there was nothing and nobody to interfere with our orgies of swimming. How old would we be? I suppose I would be about 10 and Eric eight.

But I still haven't given you the explanation of the Four Poplars. You were accepted into the swimming community of the village only after you had swum across the 20 yards or so of water that separated the trees from the Caen Meadow and had climbed at least one of them. Of course they seemed lofty and huge to my boyhood eyes, but today I'm afraid they are no longer there. Time and age caught up with them and they are no more.

When I mentioned their demise to Eric, who still lived in the village, he hadn't noticed that they were gone. He agreed with me that they had appeared to shrink, but he also reminded me that he had once climbed one of them with his father's saw and for some extraordinary reason sawn off its top branches. The silly things people find to do! Somewhere or other there is a photograph of the trees in their heyday – I must look it out.

These mighty poplars were therefore an early goal to be reached; a step, if you like, towards manhood, an achievement of arms. Here is a tale that should be told.

I think back to the year 1912 and the August of that year. Our parents were away on their summer holiday and we younger fry had been left in the care of our elder sisters and brother. In that year, my father had decided to rear his own Christmas turkey. He had hatched some turkey eggs under a broody hen and we had the care of the young gobblers. I don't suppose many people have experienced trying to rear young turkeys; I can tell you that they are the most stupid, senseless and helpless of all the creatures Noah rescued from the Flood.

The summer of 1912 was unusually wet, culminating in the great-grandparent of all thunder storms and a tremendous downpour of rain. The rain went on non-stop for almost 24 hours. Those young turkeys were a menace. Everlastingly, it seemed, had we to rescue them from rain-sodden muddy places under dripping shrubs at night, and then carry them, protesting and struggling all the way, into their shed and balance them on their perches. They were more helpless than human babies and as stupid as stupid could be, and we did not dare lose one of them. We did not do so. In spite of all the worst that the elements could do to us, we managed to rear the lot.

I can remember, after this tremendous downpour, waking up in my bedroom the following morning and clambering out of bed to see the extent of the damage the storm had caused. What I saw out of the window made me yell out to the family: "Look everybody, the river has gone! We've got a Broad at the bottom of the Caen Meadow!"

The family crowded in to look. The window of the bedroom I shared with my brother Ray was the only one that looked out over the river valley. Everyone exclaimed in excitement.

The river had risen during the night, an unprecedented thing in our flat Norfolk; it had, we learned later in the day, broken two locks further upstream and swept away the road bridge over the river at Coltishall. We had a tremendous waste of water. I remember how my four poplars stood in the midst of it all, bravely marking the geography of our part of the river.

We could scarcely wait to bolt some breakfast before we rushed out of the house, over the wires at the bottom of the garden and down the hill to the edge of the waters. The river swirled past, looking so different from our normal quiet and well-behaved stream.

The flood had arrived at fodder time. The coarse rushes and grasses cut by the local farmers were cocked and dried and then taken by river to the nearest farmstead on shallow barges. The fodder was used during the winter as bedding for the cattle in the byres. I recall fodder time so clearly; the sound of the sharpening of the scythes on the marshes, the heavy, heady smell of the mown grasses and shrubs and the carting. Two men would slip long poles while another slowly lifted the cock, almost hidden behind it, and moved it towards the barge. Watching this operation from our side of the river, it seemed more often than not that the fodder cocks were slowly sliding themselves over the surrounding rushes with no human aid. We longed to take part in this operation, but we were not allowed on the marshes beyond the actual landing spot below the four poplars.

Now those fodder cocks were floating swiftly down the river on the floodwaters. I was only six at the time, but I can clearly remember seeing hares, rabbits and squirrels sitting bewildered on the cocks as they floated downstream, wondering, no doubt, what had happened and what would become of them.

It took days for the waters to subside. The cottages at river level were all flooded and had to be evacuated. We collected all manner of débris from the banks - firewood, planks and notice boards which had been torn from their posts. My older brother and sisters rescued a rowing boat which had been pulled from its moorings, or perhaps had floated off its slipway. It was claimed by its owner, who lived in Coltishall.

When the waters had slowly drained away, there were our familiar four poplars, and we swam over to them when the elders assumed that it was safe, and marvelled at how firmly the trees had stood through all the turmoil.

The four poplars became a landmark, a symbol of these early, happy days in my home village. During the war, when I was serving in a ship far from home, I wrote these lines in the ship's magazine as I recalled my boyhood playground and the four trees.

Tall poplars rustling in the dying breeze,
Those loveliest of Godward-pointing trees,
Their shadows purple-flecked by sunset rays,
Dim-coloured glow, kaleidoscopic haze.

Tatters of tinted cloud, day's lingering flocks,
Soft whisperings in tall reeds, scented summer stocks;
Contented cattle slow peddling from their byres
As blue smoke idly curls from cottage fires.

Poplar trees were very evident on the banks of our river, from Wroxham right up the river to Belaugh, the next village above us. They were planted on both banks of the river as if to create an enormous avenue, a ploy, so we were told (although I can't vouch for the truth of it), of the village squire who was living at Wroxham Hall at the turn of the century. He very much resented his privacy being broken by the newcomers to the Broads from the yachting fraternity. Since he owned both banks of the river from Wroxham Bridge almost up to Belaugh he determined to make it almost impossible for the sailing fraternity to get any wind to fill their sails. This was, of course, well before the age of the 'infernal' combustion engine - and I mean the word 'infernal'!

The poplars, quick-growing, tall and leafy in the summer season, made an excellent windbreak. Most of them are there to this day, monuments to the age that planted them. Motorised cruisers and yachts now pay no heed to them. Those of us who welcome some privacy in these days of the ubiquitous tourist can applaud the efforts of the old Squire. When I was a boy, a row up the river on a sunny summer day was a sheer delight. One's peace was not shattered by water-hogging commercial cruisers, coxed by amateurs who regard the river as an aquatic M1.

This was very much the river of *The Wind in the Willows*, and the old squire, bless him, was trying to keep it so. My four poplars, isolated as they were by some considerable distance from their 'windbreak' brethren, must have been a last gesture of his determination to guard his privacy entire; or perhaps they were the remaining four saplings left of the last planting, and rather than throw them away, the squire's men planted them opposite the Bay as a break in the skyline.

There must have been a history attached to the Bay. Round it and in the water one could see evidence of wooden stakes, mute reminders of some earlier building – a small boathouse maybe, with a little staithe-way jutting out into the river. Perhaps there was some connection between the poplars and the boathouse. Nobody I ever knew, including the ancients of the village, with whom I talked very freely as a boy, ever gave me any clue as to an erstwhile boathouse on or near the 'Bay'.

"God grant you find one face there,
You loved when all was young".

And so in at the deep end – How did it all start?

I was on my way from Scotland to the West Country on a preaching engagement and was making a holiday tour of it, insofar as time and the distances to be covered permitted. My plan was to motor down the East Coast and out through the Fens to Norfolk to see my sisters, where I would take a look at my beloved Wroxham and the scenes of my very happy boyhood there before continuing to the West Country to fulfil my preachment.

On the first day out from Scotland, as I was some few miles south of Boroughbridge on the A1, I realised that something seemed to be amiss with the clutch of the car. It didn't appear to be serious, so I drove on cautiously until I got to my destination near Peterborough, where I was spending the night with friends. That night I took the car into the local garage. The owner could do nothing about the clutch but advised me to contact a larger garage than his, which could give me a better diagnosis of the trouble. This I decided to do.

The following morning, I set out once more on my way across the Fens, up to King's Lynn and from there on the forty-mile haul to Norwich. It was after I had left King's Lynn that the trouble re-asserted itself. I found that the taking of the few rises in the road was getting more and more hazardous (I thanked God for the flatness of Norfolk) and decided I would stop at the next 'town', which would be Swaffham, to seek out a reliable garage and ask for help and advice. I smiled inwardly as I recalled the rune of my Norfolk up-bringing:

CHAPTER ONE

"S-w-a-a-f-u-m!!
Where yu du
A days t-r-a-a-s-h-n (threshing)
For n-a-a-t-hun"

I was very lucky. The first garage I stopped at invited me to leave the car with them for an hour or so so that they could give me their verdict. I found a café, had some coffee, visited the local church, which I hadn't seen for a number of years, wandered around the shops and then returned to my garage.

There I was greeted with solemn faces. The clutch would take at least 24 hours to repair. It was a major breakdown, and required what we call in the Navy 'a dockyard refit'. The situation was far too technical for my brain to hoist in, but they clearly knew their job at that garage. It would be most unwise, they told me, to travel any further until the job was done.

I had no other choice but to take them at their word. I explained to them my itinerary and left them to it, having been told that I could collect the car at teatime on the following day. I rang my sisters in Ashmanhaugh (Ash-ma-haw), cheek-by-jowl with Wroxham, and my niece informed me that she would drive over to Swaffham and collect me in time to get me to my Norfolk destination for a late lunch. She would be about an hour.

What to do while waiting? I had already had coffee, visited the church and toured the sights, And here is where this book really begins.

Some 40 years back, I had stayed in Swaffham with some very dear friends, the local station-master and his family. Their name was Lawrence and they had, for a while, lived in Wroxham. Vaguely I knew that the daughter of the family had married and settled in or near Swaffham. It would be a rare joy to see her again, learn of the doings of her family and exchange 40 years of gossip. But the snag was that I didn't know her married name. Now, how could I find that name and discover where she lived? The local parson, of course! He would be the man who should be able to supply the necessary information, starting from the only known facts - her name had been Lawrence and the head of the household had been the local station-master.

So, to the vicarage I went. Being a parson myself, I could imagine the vicar's irritation at being hauled out of a ruri-deaconal meeting by a fellow cleric seeking the whereabouts of an old friend of 40 years back whom he knew only by a surname. To make matters worse, the vicar had only been in Swaffham for about a week, having just moved in from Norwich. However, his wife came to the rescue by stating that if anybody knew anything at all about anything or anybody in Swaffham, it would be one of the churchwardens, an elderly man who lived close by. She took me round to see him.

There was no urgency about this. I was simply satisfying my desire to fill in an hour's enforced wait by seeking out an old friend. Fortunately the churchwarden was up to the task in hand. He was immediately able to provide me with a short résumé of the Lawrence family history in Swaffham, the name of the daughter whom I was seeking, and her address. It was as easy as that.

Following his directions, I made my way to the address he had given me, which was on the outskirts of the town. There was no reply when I rang the doorbell, and my spirits sank. I tried knocking – still no reply, so I walked down a path leading to the back of the house and knocked at the back door. It opened almost at once, and there was Margaret.

Although like me she was now in her sixties, she was unmistakeable. She looked at me curiously and hesitantly, seeing my little beard, balding head, moustache and glasses. She looked at me suspiciously. "Do I know you?" she asked.

"You should do" I said. "I'm Clifford, Clifford Davies from Wroxham. Don't you remember me?"

Her face lit up. "Clifford!" she said. "After all these years! I ought to have recognised your father's eyes. I can see now, in spite of your beard and glasses and bald head - it's Clifford. Well of all things – come on in." And talking nineteen to the dozen, we went into her kitchen and through into the sitting room.

There we sat down and she told me of the years that had passed. Through photographs I met her two daughters, heard of the fortunes of the family and the deaths of her parents. She was on the brink of tears.

Then she suddenly changed the subject and talked of our beloved Wroxham. "I once took the girls down to Wroxham and we went on the river in a boat down to the Broad" she said. Her voice trembled, and she went on: "I must have put a lot more water into the river, because I had to cry. I cried buckets, I just couldn't help it. It all brought back such vivid memories of the wonderful times we'd had at Wroxham and how happy we all were. We'll never know times like that again, will we?"

"No" I said. "They were wonderful times. We had a marvellous childhood." We went on to recall some of the joys we had experienced; of the trips in Query, a quaint old barge of a boat owned by her father, in which her brothers Jack, Reggie, Bobbie and I had had great adventures. We talked of the regattas, of the village school, the church, the vicar and the various village characters. We laughed over the pranks we had got up to, the walks we had taken and all our old acquaintances, her parents, my parents, our mutual friends, organisations and village functions and affairs. Margaret really was in tears by this time, and so, almost, was I.

"You know Clifford, it was a unique village" she said. "I don't think any other place has ever been quite like it." I agreed with her; Wroxham, as we had known it, was indeed a unique village. At that moment there came into my mind the desire to recapture, for my sake and maybe for the sake of others, something of the magic of our childhood in Wroxham. This story could not be allowed to depart into the shades, unsung and unknown. I must write down what I could remember, perhaps only for my own satisfaction, but I had to write this record of a happy childhood in a unique village.

I said nothing of what I was thinking to Margaret. At last, noting the time, which had flown as it always does, while we indulging in our reminiscences, I realised that my niece would soon be arriving at the garage and would be looking for me. We parted, smiling, and I stepped out to the garage. Within a minute or so my niece arrived and we set out for Wroxham.

Like Cortes seeing for the first time the Pacific Ocean from his peak in Darien, I had suddenly caught a glimpse of a fairyland of memories. My mind was full of it all. On our way, I asked Janet, my niece: "Would you call Wroxham a unique village?"

She asked me why I had asked this. I mumbled some sort of an excuse, but repeated the question. She said that it might have been unique once, but certainly wasn't now. Yet there was something about it, she believed, that could make it match the word. She asked me why I had asked. I passed that by. We talked of other things, and spoke no more of it during my short stay with my sisters.

However, that was not the end of it. The following day I had to set out back to Swaffham to pick up my car and resume my journey west. My sisters had organised a taxi. The taxi driver confessed to being a retired policeman who had just moved into Wroxham, where he had started a private hire business. We talked of this and that, and then suddenly he said to me, à propos of nothing in particular, "Are you a native of these parts, Sir?"

I said that I had been bred and born in Wroxham and asked why he wanted to know.

"Would you say, sir," he went on, "that Wroxham could be called a unique village?"

Again that word. I was somewhat taken aback by his question, which appeared at that moment to be an invasion of my innermost thoughts. I asked him why he had made the remark. He went on to tell me that as a newcomer to the district, he had found a uniqueness (his word), that he had not found elsewhere; that – and he didn't exactly say these words, but I don't think my paraphrase of them is far out – the place and the people, that is, the 'natives', were somewhat different.

Did he like that difference? Yes, he certainly did. We gossiped on, and the more we chatted, the more determined I became to write down my memories of those happy times.

So, without any further preamble or apology for the depth of nostalgia and emotion the whole subject has awoken in my mind, I shall now plunge into my memory-bank.

CHAPTER TWO

My family

"When I was but a little tiny boy.....
"*Twelfth Night*" Shakespeare

"Oy, shut that door, it's freezing!"

A cold Friday evening in November, pre-1914. Outside, an icy blast is blowing, straight from "Greenland's Icy Mountains", or so it seemed. The blast is assaulting Wroxham in Norfolk, where I spent the first 18 years of my life. Our house caught all the winds that blew: east, south, west and north. It almost appeared in these wild gales that the winds took turns to seek refuge from their own unruliness in the peace and tranquillity of our roof.

I am having my Friday evening tub in front of a roaring kitchen range, the stove top almost red hot. Two enormous cast-iron saucepans filled with soft water from the 'tanks' (two galvanised iron containers which stored water from the catchment of the school roofs) sit simmering on the top of the stoves, the fire door of which is open, throwing a rich, warm glow on to the glistening skin of the occupant of the bath – myself, aged about three and a half, the baby of a family of six children, enjoying my Friday evening scrub.

The opening of the back door left nothing between me and the North Pole. An icy, snow-laden blast blustered its way through the open door, caressing my bare skin with Snow Queen-frozen fingers before pitting its strength against its age-old enemy, fire, before rearing up the kitchen chimney to join its fiery emissaries in the whirl of nature.

There was always a struggle to close the back door, which had an ill-fitting latch requiring, even under more temperate conditions, superhuman efforts to close cleanly. The north-westerly, sleet-burdened gale was doing its best to take possession of the house by force.

My brother Stanley had entered from the back-yard, having gained the kitchen and its comparative safety. He fought back against the rioting gale to put the latch on its 'snick'.

Dadda (we always referred to our father as 'Dadda'), always supervised the Friday-night tub for my brother Ray and me. He got up from his kneeling position by the bath, and with his added strength the final slamming of the door was effected. A wild scream from the frustrated north-westerly signalled its banishment back to its own domain. Dadda laughed and bent over the bath again, hot sponge in hand, and resumed the tale he had been telling me.

I loved to have him squeeze out the sponge, (a proper one, none of your rubber or plastic imitations in those days). I knew all about our sponge and where it came from, because Dadda had told us that it was from the bottom of the ocean, full fathom five and oooh, thousands of miles away!

In this atmosphere of kitchen, fire and steam, I feel I should introduce you to my family; after all, the greater part of this book of my childhood involves them, so you had better meet them.

Firstly there was Dadda, and I can see now his kindly, quizzical face looking down on me, his youngest child, revelling in the steaming-hot bath. I clearly recall his pleasant features, grey moustache and eyebrows, partly bald with greying temples. His eyes were grey too, grey and thoughtful and separated from each other by the top of a long Nordic nose, typical of the English North Countryman. A pair of deep laugh lines ran from the broad base of his nose, again a characteristic feature of the Yorkshireman; one of these lines was slightly lifted, giving what I can only describe as a permanent half-smile.

I can clearly remember, on the day of my paternal grandmother's funeral, seeing Dadda and two of my uncles, Shaw John and Joseph, walking together up the Church Lane, identically dressed in top hats and frock coats. I was then about three or four years old. It was only when Dadda held out his arms to me that I could distinguish him from his brothers. All shared the same greying hair, grey eyebrows sheltering the kindest of grey eyes, long Nordic noses; grey moustaches and deeply-indented laugh lines, with the characteristic beginning of a smile in one of them.

Stanley, my eldest brother, took off his hat in the kitchen, wickedly shedding some of the snow flakes down my naked back. He doffed his coat and remarked on how warm the kitchen was compared with the outside. He was then sent almost at once to fetch my brother Ray, 18 months my senior, to get ready for his bath. I was lifted out and rubbed down with a warm rough towel, my little nightshirt was put on and with an affectionate pat on the bottom I went off to find Mumma and my three sisters in the dining room.

I haven't said much of Mumma, have I? She had been, indeed still was, a beauty. She was dark and fresh-complexioned and had a tremendous sense of humour. Her ready laugh made her the best of companions. Dadda's eyes were grey and thoughtful, Mumma's dark brown and vivacious. All her children inherited those brown eyes. Mumma loved her children, and her fulsome love overflowed on to the children she taught in the school as well. She was full of good works. I suppose the greatest of these was her devotion to the Red Cross Association, which reached its peak during the 1914-18 war years, when she served devotedly as a VAD Nurse.

I can remember an event which happened in 1914, very early in the war. I was eight, and I remember that there was a terrific scare that the Germans were about to invade Norfolk and Suffolk. The threat was taken seriously by the War Office and a large defensive force was shifted into our peaceful countryside. For about 48 hours, troop train after troop train passed through our local station. They pulled in almost at five-minute intervals. I gathered that they had come from the Salisbury Plain district.

When we came out of school in the afternoon, we rushed down to the station. The village had been alerted to the needs of the soldiers. We were fascinated by the engines and rolling stock carrying the troops, types of railway transport we never seen before.

It must have been during the winter, because I remember that it was very cold and wet. Mumma and all the womenfolk she could muster had set up a depot in the waiting room on the 'downside' line at Wroxham station, and they were serving cups of tea and sandwiches to the soldiers in the crammed compartments of the trains. The officers and men were most grateful, and cheered their thanks as the trains pulled out again. Most of them, we gathered, had been travelling without any proper meals for the 200 miles or so which separated us from Salisbury Plain, with long waits at various junctions.

I remember one particular mystery on that day which wasn't solved for me until years later. Most of the locomotives hauling the troop trains were of the old GWR type, entirely different from those we knew on our local lines, the GER. As these monsters pulled into the station, I noticed that at each revolution of the huge driving wheel there was a loud and unmistakeable 'click' emanating from the engine. One never hears that sound in the diesel-electric locos of our day, and it wasn't until this last war that I found out what it was. From 1942-1944, when I was serving in the West Country, I found myself in the homeland of the engines that clicked. One day, on the platform of Exeter St David's Station, I plucked up sufficient courage to ask the driver in a stationary locomotive what the sound was.

He looked at me in a pitying sort of way, and explained. "It's the noise made by the device which exhausts air from the vacuum brake system of the train" he said. On our GER engines it was a 'chuff-chuff – chuff-chuff', on the GWR it was just a click. Fascinating, isn't it? The click is still with me in thought, and so is Wroxham Station in the rain and wind of 1914, and my dear Mumma smilingly serving out cups of tea from the waiting room on the down line platform. I expect you may hear it on the Bluebell Line, since I see that GWR 4-4-0 no. 3217 is in service there, at least according to my youngest daughter's jigsaw puzzle.

The rest of my family consisted of three sisters and two brothers, all older than me. I am the baby, and proud of it. My sisters always said I was spoiled. If I was, I wasn't aware of it. I always seemed to get the same mode of punishment as the rest, if any was handed out. I was black-haired, lively and untidy, and known as 'Johnny' or 'that boy Cliffy'. A solitary child by choice, I could amuse myself by the hour without upsetting anybody else. My brothers and sisters came down in steps from above me: first, Marjorie, my eldest sister, who was a little mother to us all. Dadda and Mumma being in school all day, Marjorie had to care for the rest of us. Later in life she took up teaching as a career, and was marvellous at it. She was a disciplinarian, strict but just, and once they got to know her, children adored her.

Marjorie possessed one great talent, the ability to get children to sing. I remember once taking a class she had trained to compete in a music festival at Woodbridge in Suffolk – that was in my teaching days. The children sang a Christmas Carol and chanted a psalm to an Anglican chant. The adjudicator was the late Roger Quilter.

Marjorie's children won hands down. Mr Quilter came over to me to congratulate me on the quality of tone and their superb performance. I introduced him to Marjorie and said "Here is their voice trainer".

"What are you doing in this part of the world, when you obviously should be in high places exercising your most wonderful gift?" Quilter asked her. But Marjorie, who was married, stayed on in her school work, lightening the lives of the children upon whom her influence fell.

After Marjorie, sister Doris. Doris always appeared to be the 'odd-man-out' in our family community. She didn't seem to fit in with our friends and confidants; Doris was one on her own, and she stayed that way. I think the only one of us who knew her really well was Dadda – but then, Dadda was the friend and tried counsellor of all who knew him, especially his children.

Victoria, Vicky to us all, comes next. Cheerful and possessed by a major measure of Mumma's sense of humour, she had in a way been an anchor of the family. While the rest of us have travelled in far lands, Vicky has remained faithful to Norfolk and stayed within breathing space of Wroxham.

Ray, who came between Vicky and me, was something of a tyrant to me. He was practical and down to earth, and ridiculed and interfered with the rather airy-fairy world in which I often lived. He would laugh at my fantasies, but Vicky always came to my rescue. To her I could turn when Ray invaded my world and threatened my security.

I have never bothered much about my personal appearance, much to the annoyance and irritation of those near to me, whereas Ray always turned out sartorially correct – even in our days at the farm, he would manage his corduroys, heavy boots and jerseys as though they were court uniform, and he got away with it, whereas 'that boy Cliffy' always looked as though he had been dragged through a hedge backwards.

On my first visit ever to the barber's chair the barber, Harry Barcham, managed to nick one of my ears with his scissors – my fault, I hated the whole process and wouldn't keep still. Blood, tears and disgrace. I have loathed all barbers ever since and have to be pushed, even now, to occupy that hated chair.

Vicky was responsible for much fun and games. She it was who provided the oak apples on Oak Apple Day, and saved vulnerable legs from stinging-nettle assaults. Even Ray, reluctantly, obeyed her dictums. Primrose Day was celebrated with its tiny posies, and Alexandra Roses would be worn on that day in high summer; on Shrove Tuesday there would be wonderful pancakes, and there was always a runaway knocker on Valentine's Eve. I can clearly remember being mystified by the knocks which sounded alternately on the back and front doors and the small gifts of chocolates and sweets which were left on the mat outside for the opener to claim. But disaster brought to an end that particular mystery, for one Valentine's Eve the excitement and fun proved too much for Vicky's enthusiasm. One of her knocks smashed the glass panel of the front door. In her excitement, she had put her fist through it. I can remember finding her in tears in the kitchen bathing a cut hand in the sink, and Mumma admonishing her for her carelessness.

And so another myth of childhood was shattered. The forces of the occult were not responsible for the runaway knocks. St Valentine withdrew into the shades with shattered glass and a bloody hand, to be followed there soon by Father Christmas.

This was my family, and such was the environment that surrounded my early years. What follows in these pages should tell of their influences in my life. Dadda had his school, his music and his choirs and all the various activities of the village, most of which he had introduced. Mumma took her place and played a full part in the village life and cared lovingly for her family.

Marjorie was Dadda's counterpart. In the years before 1924, he took on choir training with the village choirs of our neighbourhood, cycling many scores of miles with Marjorie bearing him company, enthusing bands of singers in the local church choirs and preparing them for the great Triennial Choir Festival held at three-yearly intervals in Norwich Cathedral. I remember place names like Felmingham, Salle, South Walsham and Ranworth, among many others. Going there necessitated long cycle journeys on remote and rough roads and lanes leading to still more remote places. Marjorie and Dadda never let inclement weather stop them, and anybody who has lived through a North East Norfolk winter knows well what the vagaries of the weather can do, but such was his devotion and enthusiasm that distance and discomfort never daunted them. Oil-lit bicycle lamps, rough roads, biting north-easterly winds and bitter cold were nothing compared with his single-hearted devotion to the songs of praise he so much loved.

My brother Stanley I can tell you little about. He was killed at the age of 19 in France, when I was 11. I remember him as an affectionate elder brother, dark like Mumma, long-nosed and Nordic like Dadda's family. He was loved by all who knew him, and in company with many others of his age he was mourned by the village.

Doris played on her own wicket and seemed to watch the antics and affairs of her brothers and sisters with almost Olympian detachment.

Ray had his own haunts and friends and was 'that boy' to us all. Rarely did our paths cross in pursuit of our various hobbies, interests and companions. Vicky and I trailed in the rear with our own fancies and feelings. The rest of this book, if you have patience enough to read it, will tell you of my joys and sorrows, mostly the former.

Somehow or other, great music became part of my life in those early years. Much of this was due to the influence of a man who stayed in the village and worked as a clerk to the local garage, during and after the Great War. His surname, Wightman, remains with me, and I can clearly recall his face, but any Christian name or initial has gone completely. He was a superb organist. For many fascinating hours I voluntarily pumped the bellows of the Norman

& Beard instrument in the village church, enabling him to practise (the pedals were manual, as there was no electric blower in those days). Mr Wightman became the organist at our village church and introduced us all to organ music which our former devoted lady organist volunteers could never have tackled.

I remember a setting of the *Benedicite* by a man called Naylor, in B flat if my memory serves me correctly, which needed an organist of more than average ability. I remember hearing, for the first time, the slow movement from Dvorak's *New World* Symphony and the introduction to Act III of *Lohengrin*, among many other masterpieces. Bach, Handel, Mozart, all tumbled off Mr Wightman's fingers and keys. He would quietly tell me what to listen for, and how to appreciate the gems he played. Dadda tried hard to persuade him to take me on as an organ pupil, but he would not, so my own organ prowess never advanced. I wish that he had done so. I would have given much to possess a particle of his genius and technique. The old Norman & Beard was no more than an 'off the peg' organ and had no character about it, yet Wightman made it speak like a magnificent instrument in some great cathedral.

Such then is this very short introduction to my family, as I remember them from my very early boyhood. Now that you have met them, what follows in these pages may be of greater interest to you.

CHAPTER THREE

Summer picnic

"Then, from a time which happiness made tense,
Come memories of persons long gone hence:"

The Four Poplars bring back to me so many wonderful memories. I remember an August morning with bright dawn sunshine, and the promise of it lasting. It was the summer holidays and the whole family was in holiday mood.

"It's a lovely day for a picnic up the river" said Dadda at breakfast, and wild excitement followed. Question after question was propounded, followed by suggestion after suggestion. Then one of us was despatched upstairs to Mumma to get her consent to the expedition. This was not easy to obtain, for Mumma had a wholesome, or should I say unwholesome, dislike of the water; it was something to do with a boating tragedy of years before somewhere in Yorkshire, and a girlhood friend of hers. Mumma never lived to see me become a Chaplain in the Royal Navy, with a home on the water. I'm sure she would never have known any peace of mind as long as I was at sea.

However, our pleadings and Dadda's added persuasion, coupled with an assurance from Ray and me that we would 'sit still and not rock the boat' and the combined promise from all of us to get the housework done, eventually persuaded Mumma. Ray and I followed Dadda round the house and garden like little dogs, eagerly awaiting the glorious moment when we would leave with him to fetch the boat, almost as great a treat as the actual picnic. The boat was always fetched in the forenoon so that all would be ready to set out after lunch; the picnic would be our tea. It had to be rowed some two or three miles from the boatyard to the riverbank of the Caen Meadow.

We always went to the boatyard of Mr Ernest Collins, who was a great admirer of Dadda and Mumma. To get there we had to go down Church Lane, cross over the railway bridge, cross the main road and then go 'down the Avenue'. We would take the first turning past Mr Hicks' house on the right, past the boatyard houses down the hill on the left, and there was the boatyard and the boats.

There was, of course, hanging over us the awful possibility that there might not be a boat available, and we were 'not to be disappointed' if such were the case. But somehow or other a boat was always forthcoming.

Mr Collins would greet Dadda effusively and they would stand and talk of this and that and the progress of Mr Collins' children at Dadda's school. We boys, in the meantime, having been warned by Dadda not to go too near the edge, wandered off into the delights of the boatyard, intoxicated by the compound smell of tar, varnish, paint, fresh waterweeds and fresh-cut sawdust. We might, perhaps, be allowed to step on to a yacht lying alongside one of the jetties. We would peer into the compact little cabin and wish that we were rich enough to hire such a craft and so explore Broadland.

So we wandered until we heard Dadda calling us. We rushed back to him, jumping over the mooring lines of the boats, to discover that Mr Collins had a rowboat available for us that we could have 'as long as you like, Mr Davies, as long as you like!' There was always delight on the face of Mr Collins that he could so oblige Dadda. "I can't do enough for you, Mr Davies," he would say, "in return for all that you do for my children."

A loud shout from Mr Collins for Percy or Fred or Bob would bring one of the Collins boys at the double and he would be told to 'put Nellie into the water'. Nellie was a rowboat that Mr Collins had built with his own hands for his wife Nellie, one of the sweetest ladies I have ever known. Their youngest, Olive, was my first sweetheart – we were both six at the time.

We eagerly watched Nellie being launched into the water. We were always most honoured by being sent off in so regal a craft, and the pleasure that Mr Collins experienced in letting us have it for the afternoon had to be seen to be believed. The boat in the water, cushions were produced, the varnish wiped over with a 'chammy' leather and oars put into the boat. We stepped in very gingerly, and Dadda took the oars. Mr Collins gently pushed us off and we glided into the main stream of the river.

Ray and I took it in turns to steer with the tiller ropes while Dadda rowed steadily up the river towards Wroxham Bridge, where the main Norwich road crossed the stream. We gazed at the many craft lining the banks of the river, and Ray was told to concentrate on his steering. As we approached the low arch of the bridge, Ray would have to keep his eyes peeled for other boats.

We passed John Loynes' boatyard, the pioneer yard and the oldest. Opposite his yard was the great gaunt building known as 'The Granary', a storehouse for the steam flour mill on the opposite side of the river. Ray, being 18 months older than me, always had the steering of the boat through the bridge. We would proudly wave to any of our friends who happened to be passing over the bridge as we went under. There would usually be a trading wherry or so tied up at the Mill Staithe. One or other of the wherrymen, a Bircham maybe, or a Press, would acknowledge Dadda with a wave and call out to Ray and me, "don't you git larkin' about and fall overboard!"

Ambrose Thrower's yard on the opposite bank of the river claimed our attention next. We might be lucky enough to see his steam launch Vivid getting stoked up for an afternoon trip. He too, if he happened to be about, would wave to Dadda – everyone knew 'the schoolmaster'. And so we progressed under the railway viaduct - and what heaven if it so happened a train was passing over as we went under.

Halfway along the first reach after the viaduct was the enclosure of Nobby Cocks, the local eel catcher. If he happened to be working with his cylindrical nets there was a piece of red bunting displayed, and we would pause until the nets had been safely lowered to the bed of the river so that we could pass over in safety and without damage to his gear. On the bank, we could see the large flat wooden boxes in which the live eels made their long journey by train to London, there to be transformed by the barrowboys into jellied eels and eel pies. Strangely enough I have never tasted either, although I am assured they are a rare delicacy. We always thought Nobby's craft to be fascinating and would have loved to live in such a romantic contraption as his houseboat.

Sad to relate, many years after, Nobby was returning from an evening ashore through a violent storm of thunder, rain and hail when disaster befell him. He somehow lost his bearings in the alder carr surrounding his little domain. The following morning his body was found drowned in a shallow pool within a few yards of home and safety.

Nobby was a great character. Although he caught and despatched his eels regularly to London, I doubt if he ever visited the Metropolis himself. I remember him dressed in layer upon layer of fishermen's jerseys, summer and winter alike. Fringe-bearded, apple-cheeked and always cheerful, he wore long thigh boots and fishermen's trousers. As we rowed past his plot he would wave to us, wish us a happy trip and congratulate Dadda on having picked such a fine day for an outing.

So, steadily on to the end of that reach, a wind to the left with a short reach, a turn to the right and we were in the reach called the 'Turn-Pudden Hole' or 'Turn-Pudden Bottom'. The legend of this odd name, (most of the river reaches had their own names) was told me by an old wherry skipper. Local lore had it that a Belaugh wherryman who lived with his wife in a marsh cottage close by this particular reach had a special method of warning his wife that he would soon be in for his dinner. When this old wherryman's craft was coming downstream towards Wroxham Bridge, where they always tied up for a while, the wherryman's wife would sight the large black sail of her husband's craft, recognise the design of the wind-vane at the top of the gaff – each wherry had its own design – and know that her skipper husband would soon be home for his meal. As the wherry turned the corner into Turn-Pudden Bottom the skipper would yell a "halloo" to his spouse in a stentorian roar: "Put the pudden' on, Liza!" and Liza would slap the Norfolk batter pudding which was always a staple part of the main meal into the oven, so that it would be ready for her spouse and his home-coming.

We had left the 'civilised' part of Wroxham astern of us by this time, no more bridges or boatyards for several miles. Dadda steadily pulled on, talking about this or that. Perhaps we might sight a kingfisher skimming like a shaft of blue lightning over the quiet water, or maybe a 'harnser' (the local word for heron), would rise with a harsh croak out of the reedbed and flap its ungainly way over the marshes to find a safer fishing ground. A small flock of brightly-coloured jays, uttering their harsh, unmusical cries, might break from the copse of scarlet-berried rowan trees to make for the alder or willow carrs on one or other banks. One heard their calls for some time, and there would always be a deal of fuss from the other wood-dwellers, as jays are notorious egg-thieves and no respecters of private property.

One reach followed another as we came round each bend of the river, and new views and vistas were there to be remarked on and discussed. Perchance a trading wherry might pass us on her way downstream. Civilities would pass between us and her crew of two, and the glorious morning would be extolled. Whichever of the two of us was not steering at the time would perhaps trail a hand in the water, hoping to catch a piece of floating waterweed, and would of course be warned by Dadda not to bring the weed into the boat. There is a species of waterweed which looks like a fern leaf, floating on the water and beautifully coloured. The capture of a leaf of that plant was a great prize.

Soon we would come to what I can only describe as the home stretch, a long reach, almost canal-like in its straightness, known to the wherryman as 'Ten-Acre Reach'. Whether this was the actual area measurement of the reach or whether it referred to one of the fields beyond the fringing marsh, I wouldn't know; but at the head of it, standing proudly on its little hillock as parts of it had stood in the selfsame spot since Norman times, was our village church, St Mary's.

At this point, depending on the time of the year, we would begin to hazard guesses as to whether or not Billy the swan was on the watch. Billy nested year by year in the mill dyke on the Belaugh bank of the river not far from the Caen Meadow. He patrolled for several hundred yards up and down the river in the neighbourhood of his nesting site, particularly when the pen was sitting, or after hatching when the cygnets were abroad. Billy kept at bay all whom he regarded as marauders, and that covered everybody. Anyone who came anywhere near Billy's beat was, ipso facto, a cygnet killer or nest thief and was treated as such. He was a holy terror to all the boating fraternity. We knew him and his foibles well and always gave him a wide berth, but woe betide the visitor out for a gentle pull down the river. The first warning they received would be the wild beat of Billy's powerful pinions as the swan, sighting the gate crasher, advanced to do battle. Many were the stories told about Billy's fierceness – he was even said to have broken a keeper's arm with one wing blow when said keeper had invaded Billy's privacy.

In the spring and summer when we were playing on Caen Meadow, we often heard the flurried beating of Billy's wings and would see him taking off up or down the river to warn off some innocent holidaymaker out for a quiet row. Some, terrified, turned back; others, more courageous, edged along the opposite shore from Billy, who, with head down and wings fluffed, agitated and protested more and more at these trespassers on his preserves. Woe betide anybody who neared Billy's nesting site in the sitting season. I have seen a boat attacked with flapping wings and an oar seized in Billy's powerful beak. He was both legend and reality.

Whether Billy was always the same swan or whether son followed father we none of us knew, but in spring there was always a swan on that corner of the river called Billy, nesting up the water-mill creek. He may still be there for all I know, terrorising all the inhabitants of the river and its banks. Certainly from my own earliest memories until the 18th year of my life, when we departed from the Old Schoolhouse on Dadda's retirement, Billy the swan was part of the local scene and respected as such.

And so, eventually, we would reach the Bay, where Dadda gently beached Nellie and we carefully stepped ashore. Dadda tied the painter to one of the few remaining stakes of the old staithe. Boys who were enjoying a swim promised to keep an eye on the boat, respecting 'the Master', as they called Dadda, and then the three of us would walk up the slope leading to the schoolhouse. Possibly either Ray or I would run on ahead to announce excitedly to Mumma, or any other member of the household, that we had got Nellie, and that we were home, and was dinner ready, and what time would we be starting the picnic.

Dinner over, (the word 'lunch' was not in our vocabulary), the picnic baskets were packed with comestibles – always cucumber, tomato and jam sandwiches, shortbread biscuits, seedy cake, a sponge and rock buns. A small spirit stove and kettle had to be brought down from the parental bedroom. Its ordinary function was to boil the water for Dadda and Mumma's early morning cup of tea; a bottle would be filled with milk, everything would be checked and double-checked, and when all was pronounced to be ready, we would depart with a solemn warning from Mumma that if we fidgeted in the boat or caused any trouble, it would be the last time we would ever go on a boat picnic, etc etc.

"My elders said, This was the port,
Whereto the bargeman made resort."　　*(Masefield)*

Although pundits in the world of education tell us that 85 per cent of what we learn and store in our memories during our lifetime we take in through the sense of sight, to me the sense of smell brings back more than vision can ever recall. The scent of wild mint growing in profusion along the river bank, the delightful, wistful aroma of the meadowsweet and the heady flavour of new-mown marsh grasses take me back at once to our rare summer boat picnics. We always went upstream towards Belaugh, the next village up from Wroxham, although we never got that far. Dadda wasn't all that enthusiastic an oarsman and we were too young or unsteady to be allowed to try. Besides, Mumma would never permit it. The very idea of changing seats in midstream, eight feet at the most from either bank and five feet of water beneath us, seemed to Mumma to be courting mass family suicide, so Dadda always pulled single-handed on Nellie, without any assistance.

Eventually we reached a landing place where a convenient alder tree made a good tie post, and where, if necessary and without endangering life and limb, we could clamber out on to the bank. Dadda lit the spirit stove and the kettle was put on to boil. Sandwiches were distributed, again to me in a nostalgia of smells; burning methylated spirits, cucumber sandwiches and seed cake can bring back as if they were yesterday those happy days of my boyhood, my parents, our very happy family and that paradise of my youth, the river and its surrounds.

Although it was nowhere near as busy then as it is today, there was plenty to see on the river; other boats conveying families up the river looking for suitable picnic spots, and the warm sunshine filtering down to us through the filigree lacework of the leaves and branches, the occasional passing wherry. Dragonflies with their iridescent colours, alighting on the boat and calling forth exclamations of delight. We would see Fred Pitcher rowing homewards in his fishing boat after a day's work at the Hall. A pleasure yacht would drift by, aided on its way by a skipper and his quant (pole); dabchicks would appear with their ball-of-fluff babes; a stately mute swan would come alongside our boat to take scraps of bread and the occasional crust.

At times we would hear a belated cuckoo – perhaps see it being chased by other birds, who saw it as a hawk. Not a moment of our picnic was wasted. We didn't miss anything; when tea was over no washing-up was done, although of water there was a-plenty. Everything was packed away; if there were any bits left (and there never were, save for the minutest crumbs), they were thrown to the coots or waterhens, or perhaps to a friendly swan and her cygnets. Slowly we made our way home, going with the stream back to the Caen Meadow shores. We used to sing as we went down the river, choruses like "Pull sailors, pull, pull for the shore."

At the Caen Meadow, Mumma and the girls landed and made their way up the hill towards the schoolhouse. We boys rowed Nellie back to the boatyard under the superintendence of Dadda and Stanley, not forgetting to thank Mr Collins for the use of the boat.

Tired but happy, Ray and I toddled off to bed. We shared the same bed, and in imagination, after the excitements of the day, and before sleep claimed our minds and bodies, we converted it in imagination into a huge liner. We sailed fabulous voyages. Down-the-bottom-of–the-bed, stuffily under the bedclothes, would be the engine-room. We took turns down there with the other mariner on the bridge (the pillows, of course), and the bedhead. With ding-dings and dong-dongs and the hissing sounds of mighty heads of steam; with hoarse sirens answering hoarse sirens, we put to sea – until from the bottom of the stairs would come a hail from Dadda, with both feet firmly on dry land, "All right now, you two, that's enough. Off to sleep the pair of you, or there'll be no more picnics." Warning enough; and sleep soon claimed us.

CHAPTER FOUR

The Schoolhouse

I have had playmates, I have had companions,
In my days of childhood, in my joyful school-days"

Charles Lamb

Memories of 'bedtime' remind me that I haven't yet introduced you to the schoolhouse, where I spent the first 20 years or so of my life. I was always a day boy at school, starting at about three years of age in my father's school, and then at the age of 11 going daily by train to Norwich, where I attended the City of Norwich school - the 'redcaps' as we were known, because the school colour was a vivid red.

The daily journey meant a mile's walk to the railway station to catch the 'eight train', as it was called. I can never remember being in bed after seven in the morning, unless I was sick, which was seldom. I have never yearned to 'lie in' as they say. I must be up and about.

So much for one's early habits. My family now find it irritating, but at least they are sure of a morning cup of tea in bed. Both Mumma and Dadda taught in the village school, and they had to be ready by about a quarter to nine, so there was no dawdling. I think I can honestly assert that I never remember any member of the family having to be wakened a second time.

It was only a year or so ago that I paid a visit to the old schoolhouse. It is now condemned as a dwelling place and is used for storage. The present schoolmaster told me that it would cost too much to have it pulled down, so I suppose it will be left to fall down – who knows.

I was born there during a howling gale, or so I have been told, on March

7 1906. It is a shrine of great memories for me. The room which was my birthplace, the main bedroom, overlooks the Caen Meadow to the north. I am told there was a barn in that part of the meadow viewed from the north window, but on the night of my entry into the world the gale which was my introduction took the roof off it, so the barn roof departed as I arrived.

My unkind sisters have always said that I have a temperament similar to that of the gale, but I cannot think it to be true. I am a very mild individual. Anyway, by the time I was up and taking notice, the barn walls had been pulled down and only the flint foundations of the building remained. Now even they are overgrown by the tidy-minded grass of the meadow and lost to sight.

The house was built on to the north end of the school buildings, the east side front, which was parallel to the Church Lane, our own by-road which ran from Lower Wroxham (so called in typical East Anglian nomenclature because it was the highest part of the village), down to the village church. The back of the house faced west and looked out over the Caen Meadow (of which there is much more to tell), and the flat valley of the Bure. The schoolhouse stands there still, mute evidence to the fact that the builders hadn't bothered about the light and surrounds of the schoolmaster's dwelling. It gets a touch of the sun first thing in the morning in the summer months and of course from the west in the evenings, but for the rest of the year, nary a ray lightens its windows.

During my visit a year or so back, I walked all around its empty rooms and passages. The headteacher pointed to a large damp stain on the west wall of the main bedroom. "They tried to stop that" he remarked, "and so did the Education Committee, but we couldn't. Who could live with damp like that?" He was most indignant, but I answered his question very quietly.

"We did" I said. "That damp mark was there when I was born and I can hear my parents talking about it now."

Originally the house had three bedrooms, but as the family increased the authorities added two extra rooms, one up and one down. The upstairs became the principal bedroom, the room in which I was born. The new room downstairs was known to us as the dining room. In that room we took our meals, did our homework and other chores, and here Mumma and Dadda relaxed in their armchairs after their day in school on either side of the fire.

There were other rooms downstairs, known respectively as the study, the kitchen and the drawing room. The drawing room was Mumma's showpiece, spotless and containing the piano, of great importance in our family life. It hoarded pieces of Goss china, mostly displayed on a true Victorian what-not with souvenirs of visits, visitors and holidays. The drawing room was sparingly used and then only with hushed feet and voices (except when singing, of course), but the jingling of the Goss would always give you away when you entered the room. If the drawing room was taboo - perhaps in the aftermath of spring cleaning, or the advent of some visitor - no matter how softly one tried, there would be a jingle from some irritating piece of Goss and Mumma's voice from somewhere in the house, "Who's that in the drawing room? What are you doing?" One would then make one's excuses and retreat.

The carpet had a strip of 'drugget' leading from the door to the piano stool, to protect said carpet, of course, and the upright piano had a stop or damper at the right-hand end of the keyboard. This cut down the noise made by the piano when practice was in progress. It was very effective, though I don't remember ever having seen such a device on any other instrument.

Finally there was the kitchen, a small room containing the sink for washing up, a ramshackle coal-fired kitchen range (which I have mentioned before), and two larders, one under the stairs and the other by the back door, which opened out into the backyard and the pump for the fresh water – and beautifully fresh it always was. The larder was infested, I remember, by ants, and foodstuffs had to be insulated from their wanderings.

Upstairs there were four bedrooms and a box room called the bathroom. It had neither bath nor water laid on, hot or cold. The parental bedroom I have already described: the back bedroom had the best view from its small window, out towards the west over the Caen Meadow with its trees and bushes, the river and the marshes. Away in the distance between the trees, one could glimpse Wroxham Hall, home of Squire Trafford, with a flag flying when he was in residence.

The window looked towards the setting sun and the woods on the shallow hillside on the farther side of the river. These woods, all the year round, housed large congregations of rooks. Their comings and goings from their feeding grounds and their wild whirlings over their sleeping billets were our 'last post' at nightfall. In the winter months they roosted there after 'singing' Evensong, as we put it. It was almost antiphonal in its arrangement. I wrote some verses about it during the war, which went something like this:

"Vast choirs of rooks sing feathered Evensong

Then settle noisily to sleep where rooks belong."

The side bedroom looked towards the north. One could see the church from it and the house of our nearest neighbour, Holly Lodge, the home of the village blacksmith and his family. Eric Stevenson whom I have mentioned before, lived there, the baby of that family. He was my earliest playmate, and we still keep in touch. It seems a very long time ago since we played together on the Caen Meadow and down Church Lane, and a deal of water has flowed under Wroxham Bridge since then.

The other bedroom was the girls' room, occupied by my three sisters. It was next to the school buildings and looked to the east. I ought to have mentioned that from the bed in the side room, through the window and the trees outside, one could see the red/green light of the distant down signal for Wroxham Railway Station, and we used to watch for it in the winter months after we had gone to bed, to see the red turn to green herald the approach of the last train from Norwich on Saturday evenings. Amber as the distant signal light had not then been introduced.

The last train from Norwich used to bring our parents home from their weekly shopping expedition. They had a one-mile walk home from the station, so it was some 20 minutes or so before we saw their 'bulls-eye' lantern coming up Church Lane and heard their entry into the house and their enquiry as to whether or not we were asleep (we never were). If our elder brother and sisters gave a report of good behaviour on our part, some treat or other would be brought upstairs to us.

We must have been Spartans in our ability to stand up to the elements. North East Norfolk is a cold spot and the schoolhouse faced north. When a wild winter north-easterly blew in over the flat lands, there was nothing, as Dadda always said, "between us and the North Pole". We had neither gas nor electricity, and it wasn't until after the 1914-18 war that we got an oil stove. Water had to be pumped into a pail from a well in the yard at the back of the house. The 'loo' was about 30 or 40 yards from the house, and answering (as Dadda always so politely put it) a 'call of nature' through a blizzard, snow, rain or frost was an ordeal not dissimilar from that experienced by Eskimos under similar conditions.

I have often felt that Apsley Cherry-Garrard in his saga of Antarctica, The Worst Journey in the World, could have found a good acclimatisation training ground at the old schoolhouse at Wroxham in the early part of the 20th century. All water for the house had to be pumped from the well and carried indoors, and kindling had to be prepared the night before to light the kitchen stove for the cooking of breakfasts in the morning. A double saucepan of porridge was always left on the stove so that it cooked overnight and needed only to be warmed up in the morning. All housework had to be completed by 8.45 am, since Dadda and Mumma both had to be in school by that time. We children all had our allotted tasks. Mumma was a house proud Yorkshire woman, and nothing was skimped. Literally, one could have eaten one's meals from the spotless floors.

Mumma did all her own laundering, helped by a good wife from the village. The washing was always done on a Tuesday ('hash' day for dinner), come rain come high water. Ray and I had to fill the copper in the wash kitchen and two baths. The copper was a large one and the carrying of full buckets across the yard to the wash-kitchen was no light task. In the winter and spring when rain was plentiful, the water was drawn from two large zinc tanks which were a catchment for rain from the school roofs, but in the summer when rain was scarce the water had to be pumped from the well. That was a labour indeed, but no amount of grumbling would free one from the burden. Sometimes Stanley, our elder brother, would take pity and help us, but that wasn't often. He had his own jobs to do. I remember too as I got a little older, say eight or nine, being roped in at playtimes on Tuesday mornings to turn the mangle for the washing. How I hated that chore! Still, doing those routine, boring jobs stood me in very good stead. It was then that I began to cultivate a mental state which allowed me to escape from the grinding dullness of the physical chore into another world, the world of the imagination, where fantasy would play a large part and fairyland wasn't far removed.

We fed simply but hugeously. What I mean is that apart from the occasional birthday, Christmas etc, our food was good and wholesome, but there were no frills or fancies. There was a garden, which was cultivated for green and root vegetables and a certain amount of fruit. Dadda, being a townsman by birth, was no great shakes as a gardener, but needs must; money was scarce and the home-grown garden stuff filled hungry tummies. Before 1914 the combined salaries of my parents amounted to £120 a year (with, of course, a free house) and we had to be fed and clothed from that, yet somehow our parents managed to get us a week by the sea in the summer. They had to be good managers, and they were. We never went hungry.

I think a great deal of our family happiness came from our singing Yorkshire parents, both sprung from musical families, who produced musical children. I can never remember learning to read music - it seemed to come naturally to me - but I can tell you that at the age of six I could read at sight and sing any of the parts, in my treble voice of course, in an SATB (soprano/alto/treble/bass) arrangement. I remember Dadda demonstrating this ability of mine to my godfather; he wouldn't take my father's word for it, so a hymn was picked out at random, one I didn't know. I was given the key note from the piano, and without accompaniment I sang, non-stop, all four parts one after the other. I can see my godfather's face now – and feel the sixpence he gave me.

We sang every Sunday evening after tea in the drawing room clustered round the piano, mother or one of my sisters playing, and between us putting in the four parts. We loved to sing unusual hymns, those not generally heard in churches. I have often felt that I would like to present a radio programme of such a singing session. There are some really marvellous hymns and tunes which are never heard.

Dadda and Mumma sometimes, when they were in the mood, caused us a deal of amusement by singing real old Victorian and Edwardian 'lover' duets that they had sung in their courting days. I am humming one of them, called *When the wind bloweth into the sea from the sea*, as I type these words, and now another, *Oh that we two were maying*. I don't think, in fact I am sure, that I have ever heard either of them sung anywhere else since. And, of course, this singing habit spread through the village. How could it help but do so, with such enthusiasts as my beloved parents as the inspiration?

The BBC TV children's programme *Bill and Ben the Flowerpot Men* always began with the storyteller saying "and there they all are, sitting in the warm sunshine." It is a funny thing, you know, Norfolk is a bleak and flat county, but it is also a rain-shadow area. My memories of Wroxham are mostly concerned with fine weather. We seemed to have much more sunshine than rain, and when I think of the garden at the old schoolhouse, I see it in sunshine – hot sunshine – the paths round the house and down the garden a soft dust, hot like the desert sands in the summer weather. Dadda was no great gardener, as I have said, but we had to grow our own fruit and vegetables to augment the larder.

I do remember so clearly the apple trees. At one corner of the garden there grew what must have been a Bramley seedling, a wonderful tree for fruit. Dadda knew nothing of pruning, spraying or whitewashing, yet year by year the 'cooking-apple-tree', as we called it, gave us ample fruit for dumplings, pies, 'jacks' and what-not with sufficient fruit left over to donate to the Harvest Thanksgiving, as well as enough to wrap in newspapers and store carefully in old tin trunks in the wash kitchen to last us until the following Easter.

At the bottom of the garden grew two Blenheim orange trees, which again never seemed to fail us. These fruit were also for storage, but we children savoured their sharp tang even before they ripened.

I am leaving the queen of the trees to the last, a July apple; I can't guess the variety, but it was the sweetest and most succulent apple I ever tasted. Again, it bore prodigiously. We were allowed free access; there was always plenty of fruit, and if we didn't get it the wasps would. To pick an apple straight from the tree on a sunny day! It was not only sweet and juicy but warm to the taste and always a beautiful greeny-red. Even before they were mature, those apples were sweet. The tree still stands in the same corner of the garden and still bears fruit. I saw it last year, ancient, venerable, moss-hung, and, dare one say it, looking a little weary. It appeared to have the same shape too, and I was told its apples still have the same engaging sweetness.

In that same corner of the garden stood our hen-house, known to us as The Gables. I can remember it being delivered to us just before the First World War, with its run and chickens. We possessed the usual belligerent cockerels and one extremely bat-witted hen called Auntie (it was supposed to resemble one of our aunts, but I never knew which). This hen was as soppy an animal as I have ever seen – a veritable ninny of a chicken. The stupid hen would come when called – "Arny, arny, arny!" - and the fool would come and squat down in the dust to be stroked.

At one period in its history, the Gables and its feathered denizens became rat ridden and Dadda had to fetch in the local ratcatcher and his ferrets and fox terrier. Ultimately the house had to be moved to allow us freer access to the rats. The floorboards had long since gone. Dadda took command of the operation and we children were all ordered inside to get a convenient hold on the framework and to lift it and walk when told. The order was given and we all lifted. It was too much for us. There wasn't room to breathe, let alone walk, and then the funny side of the thing hit us and we collapsed.

Dadda got cross. The more commands he gave, the funnier we thought it was. Eventually we were so convulsed with laughter, verging on hysterical, that we found it quite impossible to support the weight of the Gables, and the whole operation came to a grinding halt. We dropped it and trooped outside to see what was happening. When we saw the shambolic state of our hen house, it was just too much. Helplessly we staggered about, laughter-tears streaming down our dirty cheeks. Dadda was very cross, and said so, so we all piled inside again and this time we completed the move. The rats were unearthed and caught amidst scenes of mayhem, blood and excitement, and then came the awful business of putting the house back. It was as hilarious a business as before. Eventually we emerged helpless with laughter to find ourselves in dead trouble with Dadda for the rest of the proceedings. He couldn't stomach what he called 'silliness'.

There was also a plum tree in the garden, old and neglected. It produced little round plums and very few of them. One climbed the tree to get at them and they were hardly worth the climb. In the opposite corner of the garden near the Bramley was a sumac tree, aged, venerable and climbable. With its almost tropical foliage, it became my venue for playing Coral Island or Swiss Family Robinson games.

But I had better leave the garden for the nonce and look at the rest of the schoolhouse 'sitting there in the warm sunshine'. There was 'down the sheds', some steps across the yard leading down to the wash kitchen and the coal shed, the latter being the home of generations of toads, from ancient and wart-strewn great grandfathers to the newest and smallest of the hoppers. I remember them most distinctly as being part and parcel of the school surrounds. Although it was next door to them and they had free access, they never invaded the wash kitchen. This, I should imagine, was because the long war carried on against them by Mumma must have penetrated their leathery hides. At any rate, one never saw them in that sanctuary of cleanliness.

Behind these two sheds, solidly surrounded with brick and tile, was a kind of wasteland, not very large, which was really the backyard. This was my stamping ground for my own games. It was bound on three sides by the back walls of sheds, while its other side lay open to the Caen Meadow over some loose wires, which just served to keep the cattle out of the schoolhouse surrounds. The ground outside the railings sloped steeply down into a large hollow, the remains of what must once have been a large sandpit. There was a wonderful sand hole close by with the most marvellous clean sand. We played there from time to time, but only when Mumma was out. It brought far too much sand into the house on our clothes and boots.

In the centre of this small backyard was a four-square line post, main anchor for the Tuesday washing line, and this became on windy days the mainmast of my imaginary fishing smack, schooner, brig, or what have you. I sought out a forked pole and searched the outhouse until I came across a fairly clean sack. I split this open and fastened it loosely to the post, and made the shape of a boat from old school benches, along with any other planks handy. The wind blowing over the valley from the prevailing land of winds, the south west, filled my improvised sail, and Treasure Island, Robinson Crusoe and Coral Island all came to life.

I am remembering now my very early years, when, as a baby, I had to amuse myself quite a bit, and I can so well remember with a nostalgic happiness the hours and hours I spent in my 'sailing boat', sitting in the warm sunshine, looking down to the river and its wherry craft and my four poplars, and yearning for the time when I could be old enough to go with the other boys on a real boat on the river, to cross over and climb them.

"Every minute dies a man
And one and one sixteenth is born"

But before leaving home and the cherished memories of those early days, I feel I must record two or three incidents that stand out particularly clearly in my memories of the school house. Stanley, my eldest brother, who was killed in France as a private serving in the Lancashire Fusiliers in 1917, was a wonderful elder brother to us. I was only 11 when he gave his life at the early age of 19. I can remember vividly that awful morning when the news of his death arrived in the house.

Unfortunately the news preceded the official telegram by some days. Mumma, in addition to her teaching duties, did part-time nursing with the Red Cross Association, which great organisation ran a convalescent home, St Gregory's in the village. From grateful soldiers who had been nursed by her and her fellow workers, she would receive letters from all parts of the front by practically every post, so that when one arrived on this particular morning in the familiar service envelope, possibly with one or two others, no one took any notice.

The letters went upstairs on Mumma's breakfast tray (she had been on night duty and hadn't long been home), and it was only when we heard Mumma calling Dadda from upstairs, and the note of fear and urgency in her voice that we realised something was amiss. Galvanised into action, we rushed up the stairs at the heels of Dadda, to be greeted at the bedroom door by a distraught Mumma with the dreadful news of Stanley's death.

A friend of his had written. He had been with Stanley walking along a communication trench when a highly explosive shell had burst close by and a splinter of steel had killed our brother outright.

Mumma had received the news first, and the whole shock of it had hit her badly. It was a terrible morning. Dadda had to go into the school and dismiss the children, having first telephoned the Education Office in Norwich and obtained permission. The children were as shocked as we were. Embarrassed and hushed, they drifted away from school to their homes, bearing the gloomy news with them.

I remember going off to the Caen Meadow on my own to digest this first encounter with death. The Chamberlins at the Post Office had lost three sons, and the Wrights, the Bemans and many others had suffered. We had grieved with them. Dadda had taught those boys, and now this had happened to us. I remember sitting down by the river on my own, thinking about Stanley, about life and death and the mystery of it all. I recalled the way he used to organise wonderful games for us, cowboys and Indians, goodies and baddies.

I remember so clearly one particular piece of nonsense. It must have been when Stanley was about 15, having left school for the wide world, and it was a Saturday, just after Guy Fawkes' Day on November 5. Mumma and Dadda had gone into Norwich as usual and Stanley and the girls were left in charge of Ray and me. There had been general command to do a bit-of-clearing-up in the garden. Ray and I were enrolled by Stanley to help, and, typical of Stanley, the whole ploy developed in to a tremendous game of cowboys and Indians. As we uprooted long rows of pea-sticks and bean-sticks, instead of tying them in faggots as we knew we should have done, Stanley told us that we were about to be attacked by a tribe of hostile Indians and that we hurriedly had to build a stockade. Eric and Stanley Stevenson, the blacksmith's sons from Holly Lodge, heard our excitement and laughter and bustled over to see what was happening. They stayed on to join the fun. We lit a bonfire inside our stockade, and with the blacking of our faces with the ashes from the fire, the hot potatoes, the noise and the fun, nobody heard the last train from Norwich go down. Mumma and Dadda were home and among us before we had time to scatter. We were grimy, it was nearly nine o'clock and we two little 'uns should have been in bed hours before.

Poor Stanley and the girls got fleas in their ears, while Ray and I scattered for a quick wash and bed. Mumma and Dadda were very cross with us, but what a game we had enjoyed! It was worth all the wigging.

Later on Stanley came upstairs and we managed to let him know what a wonderful time we had had. We hoped Dadda and Mumma weren't too cross with him and he whispered that it was all right and we were to go to sleep, which we did, after we had eaten the bread and cheese he had smuggled up to us. I suppose we dreamed wildly of a mixture of Indians, cowboys, potatoes and the rest of it.

I remember another curious phase I went through in those early years. Whether or not, at that time, I was a solitary child, I don't know. The fact is that I did, and do now, live rather in a world of my own, needing no company in my fantasies. I wasn't, nor ever have been, anti-social; it was just that I enjoyed my own Never Never Land.

It was about that time that Mumma and Dadda had taken us, a rare treat, to see a touring company play *Peter Pan* at the Theatre Royal in Norwich – my first ever visit to a theatre. I was at once at home both in the theatre and in the fantasy world of J M Barrie. It was that sort of world that I enjoyed and loved. It was a phase which made me seek out or create my own 'familiars' – that is the only name I can give them now, after almost 60 years. I had a small negroid figurine which had been given me by a lady who had it left over on her stall after a Missionary Bazaar. This small piece of bric-a-brac, rather like an ashtray (it was made of lead), was painted with a little palm tree, and under the palm was the small figurine. I suppose the whole thing was supposed to represent an oasis. I was delighted with it. Burbling a 'thank you ever so!', I went off outside to examine my prize. The little figure came away from the dish in my hand – I think he must have been screwed to the base. Here, to hand, was my 'little man' – I immediately gave him that name. He was to be my confidant; to live in my pocket, to share my Never Never Land and all my secret thoughts. The family soon noticed it and chaffed me about it, but it made no difference. I had my friend, 'closer than hands or feet, nearer than breathing', or so it seemed to me. My little man was my heart's joy for several weeks; not longer, for I lost him, and even now I can feel the pain, bewilderment and sense of loss.

It was a sunny day, warm and comfortable, and I was by myself on the Caen Meadow with my companion. I was playing with him and teaching him how to climb up the post of the field gate. As I reached up with him, my foot slipped and he jerked out of my hand and seemed to slip down between the gatepost and the wall. He just disappeared. There was plenty of space between the post and the wall for me to get my hand down to feel and to explore, but I couldn't find him. I looked for him for so long that I was late for tea and was scolded, but after tea I went back out again and searched until almost dark. He couldn't be far away, but he was gone. I searched for weeks, alone always because I couldn't bear to share my sense of loss with anybody else. He was gone, and I never saw him again. During those years, I suppose between the ages of five and seven, I had many other 'familiars', but none ever approached the strange attachment that I had to my first 'little man'.

One final nostalgia for the old schoolhouse. It is of the week following 'Stir Up Sunday', the Sunday next before Advent, as the Book of Common Prayer so nicely has it, when the Collect of the day starts: 'Stir up O Lord the wills of thy faithful people'. This is the week when the plum puddings and mincemeat were made. On a suitable evening, usually a Tuesday or Wednesday, we all solemnly gathered round the dining-room table, Dadda at one end and Mumma at the other, and we children seated in our proper places, Ray on Mumma's left, me on her right, next to me, Doris and then Victoria. On the opposite side was Ray, then Marjorie, and next to Dadda, Stanley. That was how we always sat at mealtimes, and it was awful when we got the giggles. It used to infuriate Mumma, but Dadda, while telling us to behave and be quiet, always had a twinkle in his eye. Many's the time I have been banished to the kitchen – "Come back when you know how to behave!" would be Mumma's parting shot. If Ray or I had been rebuked by Mumma, which she often enforced by a sharp clip on the ear, I can remember his complaint that it wasn't fair. He always got the worst of it because he would get Mumma's left hand with her ring finger. I got the plain hand.

Returning to our pudding making, Mumma always produced the recipes, which never changed, year in year out. They were Yorkshire ones which had belonged to her great granny, and they were written on faded paper in faded ink. They were followed very seriously. Stanley weighed the ingredients according to instructions, when they were tipped into the big mixing bowl. It was in the days before shredded suet, stoneless raisins or cut peel. We younger fry had our jobs stoning raisins and sultanas and the like. Dadda had an enormous wooden mortar with a vicious semi-circular knife like a miniature guillotine blade, with which he chopped suet, apples, peel or whatever came his way. Our sisters kept an eagle eye on Ray and me to see that we didn't eat too many of the raisins we were stoning. A great reward was to share the delicious sugar that came from the centre of the candied peel, to get a slice of apple from Dadda's mortar, and from time to time to share in the stirring of the mixture in the huge bowl.

Making puddings and mincemeat for our large family took the whole of the evening, after the tea things had been washed up and put away and it ended in another grand wash-up. Plans were made for the boiling of the puddings the following day, and the evening would end in chatter, bread, cheese and cocoa. Dadda talked to us of how the Christian family was composed and about the various lands from whence had come the exotic fruits of the earth for our good cheer.

Sometimes, if it was a fine night and not too late, we three boys were allowed outside to fill the copper for the boiling of the puddings on the following day, and we never grumbled at that chore. Eventually the evening closed, and Ray and I would stagger up to bed happy and contented in the wonderful family warmth engendered by the occasion and looking forward to Christmas, which seemed now only just round the corner.

CHAPTER FIVE

The Caen Meadow

*Tuesday, Midsummer Day 1873: "Walter Brown of the Marsh says
that his grandfather once saw some fairies in a hedge. But before he could get down
out of the cart they were gone!"*

I have already mentioned that magnificent field called the Caen Meadow,
which stretched from the Church Lane, our local by-road, down to the River
Bure, its western boundary. To the north, the long garden of Holly Lodge,
the blacksmith's domain, bordered it, and to the south, the gardens of cottages,
Sot's Hole and the Public Staithe. The south-east corner of the meadow had
at one time been a large sandpit, about which I have already written. A fair
sized chunk of it had been bitten off on the south-east corner for the grounds
of the school and the schoolhouse. It was not common land, although one
feels that at one time it must have been, since the villagers have always
regarded it as their recreation ground. Indeed, today the present Squire seems
to have accepted that viewpoint, as there is a notice on the gate announcing
to all and sundry that the field 'may be used by the villagers for their
recreation'.

'Spider' Howlet, who, in my infancy was tenant of the Meadow and used
it for grazing his cattle, never regarded it as a playground; in fact I can still
hear his stentorian voice echoing over the hollow left by the old sandpit as
he bawled from the balcony of the farm house of the Hill Farm at the top
end of Skinner's Lane.

"Hey! Hey! Hey! You boys! Git you out of that sandhole! I'll be down
there wit my whip if you don't get a move on and git out of my medda!

You'll be breaking my cow's legs with them there holes you're a-diggin' on!"

One or two of us would have been playing innocently in the small sandhole close to the railings of the schoolhouse, and Spider took this in very bad part. We scattered to the cover of the bushes, or over the wires to the haven of home, but Spider's bark was far worse than his bite. He it was who used to give all his farm workers the day off on Good Friday, on the understanding that they attended church that morning. They all turned up in their Sunday best, usually preserved for weddings and funerals. They would stand outside the church porch in their dubbined best boots, looking slightly awkward and out of place, accompanied by their wives and families, who were quite at home. We were a worshipping community at Wroxham. As soon as the service was over they doffed their Sunday best and were off to their gardens and allotments, when traditionally they planted their potatoes. As one of them remarked: "Stands to reason, ya know. The good Lord, he was put in the ground on Good Friday and he come up all right, and so will my 'taters!"

Why this particular field was called Caen Meadow I have never discovered; laziness on my part perhaps, but then it wasn't until I visited Wroxham a few years back and saw the legend on the gate about its availability for village recreation that I even knew the correct spelling of it. We were always taught in the village school that it was 'Cane Meadow', and in our compositions on our village and its history and life, we were always instructed that it bore the title 'Cane' because it was used to store the thatching reeds from the surrounds of Belaugh Broads, just over the river and the marshes, and that the wherries would call at the staithe at the north-west corner of the meadow to collect them.

Patently this was not true, and our teachers had got hold of the wrong end of the stick. So far as I can now gather, the name has a much wider significance. The main doorway of Wroxham Church consists of a magnificent Norman archway with some of the original colour showing on it. I am told that the church, of which this porch is the only remainder, had been built by monks from the great abbey of Caen in France, and in some way or other, the Caen Meadow is linked with those ancient builders.

Certainly it seems to me the most feasible explanation of the name, because in all my youth I never remember seeing any thatching reeds cut from the marshes around us, nor a cargo in wherries down the river from our staithe. In any case, Norfolk thatching is called 'reed thatching' and 'cane' is no part of it.

The Caen Meadow, from our point of view as children, was divided up into three very definite sections. These were known as the Sloes, a covert of sloe or blackthorn bushes covering that part of the meadow closest to the school grounds; the Bushes, bramble bushes, which covered the opposite sides of the old sandpit from the sloes; and the Meadow, which comprised the rest of the field. It was really quite large and a wonderful playground. The Sloes covered a fairly steep and large slope down from the school boys' playground, sheltered by the 'Plantation' and running down to a small grassy clearing which narrowed into a path past two elderly, but very climbable, red-blossomed may trees and from thence down to the river. It was a wonderful terrain for Tarzan games and elementary climbing practice, for the trees were nowhere more than 10-12 feet high.

The Bushes covered the other two slopes of the old sandpit and were dense thickets of brambles, a harvest ground for jam-makers or just hungry kids, as we were in the blackberry season. Years of usage of these bushes for their fruit had made a definite pattern of pathways through them, which summer by summer were carefully trodden out anew as succeeding generations of pickers pursued the luscious fruit. These wild blackberries were superb. I have never tasted better.

The rest of the meadow included the field bordering the river, where in summertime we bathed. Our garden at the schoolhouse opened directly on to the Caen Meadow, and it was our paradise as boys – and girls, of course, for they shared it with us. In summer there was swimming, fishing, boating and all that the river could supply to occupy our leisure hours. In winter there were games in the bushes and 'down the sloes'. When snow graced the meadow and changed our world to glistening white, out came the sleighs and the gentle slope down that part of the meadow nearest the bushes made yet another adventure for us in the biting cold, ending with wild games of snowballs and rolling in the snow.

We were never bored in the Wroxham of which I write. That description given to me by the taxi driver that it was a unique village was right, and I can't help feeling that much of this sense of uniqueness centred on the Caen Meadow. I repeat, we were never bored. My father had moved to Wroxham on his marriage to my mother in 1891. Townsman though he was by upbringing, he and Mumma had adapted themselves wonderfully to village life. It was primitive when I was a little boy there, but in 1891 it must have been much more so to an urban-bred young couple, used all their lives to gas, tap water and all the amenities of town life. To have to struggle with our old kitchen range, to clean and care for the paraffin lamps which were our illumination in the wintertime, plus all the isolation of the countryside after the closeness and cosiness of life in Sheffield must have taken pluck and long suffering. Yet I never heard either of my parents grumble about it.

Dadda's school was the model of a village school. Not only was he headmaster and teacher, the children were his life. That is why I stated that we were never bored; he always saw to it that boredom lay outside our experience, and this not by his bossiness or 'leadership' (as modern youth workers will call it) but by an influence and inspiration that permeated our lives without knowing that he was the source of it all. He had a wonderfully expressive voice for reading aloud, and every Friday afternoon after playtime he would settle the top classes of the school down to be read to. And what reading! There was Tom Brown's Schooldays, The White Company, The Talisman, David Copperfield, Treasure Island, Westward Ho!, Swiss Family Robinson, King Solomon's Mines and scores of other classics which I still enjoy and read again and again. Lorna Doone comes to mind. It was a great favourite of his. I can hear Dadda's voice ending a chapter one Friday afternoon, the one describing the first visit of Tom Faggus to Plover's Barrows Farm. The chapter ends 'and Betty Muxworthy roaring in the wash-up'. We all felt that we were there, and left school after prayers roaring with laughter, not at, but with the Ridd family, and 'Betty, roaring in the wash-up'.

Who could ever be bored, with such wonderful adventures constantly in our minds and thoughts? The Sloes, the Bushes, the Meadow, the river, enabled us to translate all these adventures into practical games. We were the White Company, the pirates, the crusaders, the schoolboys at Rugby. Incidentally, talking of Tom Brown's Schooldays, it is only recently I have realised, on re-reading the book, one of the results of Dadda's choice of literature for us; we were never at a loss for something to do. There was no juvenile delinquency in our village; we never had time for it. If we weren't at school, at church, choir practice, Scouts or some other such ploy, we were playing one of our games, one of the games originally taught us by Dadda and transmitted on to us by the generation immediately ahead of us.

We played games in our spare time such as I have not witnessed elsewhere, and these games Dadda must have read in Tom Brown, looked up and taught to us. Each game produced its own natural leadership. Turning back to Tom Brown, do you remember how Tom was allowed by the Squire, his father, to mix with the village boys after school, and the list of the games they played? There were "Prisoner's Base", "Rounders", "High-cock-a-loram", cricket, football and many others. These were the games we played too, and we didn't quarrel about them. There was a wonderful sportsmanship and honesty about it all. I realise that all this may sound a kind of boy's Utopia. Be that as it may, it was our life. Just imagine playing games of "I-Spy", or "Touching out of home" among our sloes and bushes, 'Pirates' on the river and among the alder carrs on the marshes, 'Westward Ho!' on the Spanish Main (our river) and 'Swiss Family Robinson' over the whole of our terrain. Mark you, we were by no means paragons of all the virtues: we had our ups and downs, our scrapes and apple scrumpings and all the rest of it. We certainly fell out with the farmer folk and the keepers in some of our wilder adventures.

I remember very clearly one such adventure, and it makes me chuckle even now, some 50 years on. It concerned Ray and me, Stanley and Eric

Stevenson, Sidney Read and Apples Coffin. The game was, I think, Treasure Island, but that day we had no boat since Eric's father had taken their boat pike fishing. Then Sid Read, who lived just above the marshes by the church said that Ikey Tooley, one of the local small farmers, had borrowed one of the Squire's fleet of shallow-draft barges to transport some fodder from upriver down to his farm. The lighter, so it was reported by Sid, was tied up in a small creek off the main stream and was 'ripe for the plucking'. Sid added the most important bit, ie that to the best of his knowledge and belief, Ikey Tooley, the farmer concerned, had gone with his missus in the dog cart to Norwich Market. Sid had seen him go that morning. It was therefore quite safe, according to Sid, for all of us to board the fodder barge and yo ho ho, off we'd go in the lighter for the Spanish Main.

Cautious Apples did remind us that Ikey had threatened to put a horsewhip behind any of us that he saw either (a) trespassing on his marshes or (b) daring to touch any of his property, with special emphasis on the lighter. But we took no notice of Apples – he had the reputation among us as being a 'windy britches''. Anyway we reconnoitred the farm and its ancillary buildings and having found no sign or trace of Ikey, or his spouse, we sneaked off down to the creek to man the lighter.

On the way, the parts in the prospective drama were wrangled over and settled. Stanley was to be Captain Smollett, Sid Doctor Livesey, Apples Long John Silver, Ray Squire Trelawny and Eric Jim Hawkins, while I was the bloodthirsty Israel Hands. We furbished various weapons from the long willow wands growing along the carr and boarded the vessel. We slipped our moorings, and taking up the quants, or poles – there were two of them - with many yo-ho-hos and shouts of 'give way, me hearties' we pushed ourselves into midstream.

Our Norfolk rivers meander very lazily through the flat country. There is little or no current under normal conditions, so poling the lighter either way, up or down stream, presented no problems. We were having a whale of a time, plenty of room to move about on the decks and a fine stage for the high adventure of the seas. Nothing ventured, nothing gained, so we decided to forsake the short reach we were manoeuvring in and go further afield, down the river a bit to Ten Acre Reach. There was open water and lots of it, so down the midstream we pushed and shoved. I have an idea that at about this stage of the proceedings the game changed from 'Treasure Island' to 'Westward Ho!', so we kept a watch out for Spanish galleons loaded with treasure from the Indies. Spying in all directions, with no other ships in sight, there was suddenly a shout of dismay from windy-britches Apples.

There on the bank by the creek from which we had taken the lighter was Ikey Tooley, plus whip, and plus, by the gesticulations and odd cries floating down the river, a hearty desire to do us no good at all. He was clearly very, very cross. Hastily we pushed into the opposite bank from the approaching Ikey, and took a council of war. All our imaginative playing was now a matter of grim earnest, aimed at the avoidance of that menacing horsewhip which we knew Ikey would not fail to use. Stanley Stevenson and Ray, our natural leaders in all these ploys, said that there was only one answer to it all. We must give the lighter a shove out into midstream and make our way along the opposite bank until we got to the Four Poplars opposite the Bay. There we would strip to the buff, wrap our clothes into bundles and hold them high above our heads until we gained the comparative safety of the Caen Meadow. As for the lighter – well, that would drift slowly downstream, possibly to finish up along the far bank. We guessed, correctly, that Ikey would be far more concerned to salvage the lighter than to catch us. He would be thinking that we could keep to another day. He knew who we were.

So the lighter was given a good push into midstream and we set off towards the Four Poplars for our short swim to safety. Another hazard had to be passed before we reached the trees – the mill-dyke, as we called it. On the corner where normally Billy the swan held jealous sway there was a functional windmill which pumped water off the marshes and emptied it into the river.

The mill was owned and controlled by a Belaugh farmer, Mr Ives. He too had it in for us, because we had been known to interfere with the mechanics of the mill, swinging the sails into the wind and risking much damage to the simple mechanism. He had never caught us at this ploy, but always there was a watch kept when the mill was functioning lest we dare try it again. We had to get to the mill, which was about 50 yards inland, and negotiate the rickety bridge that crossed the mill dyke, without being seen. Fenimore Cooper's The Deer Stalker became our new game, and we stalked past the mill (pretending we were in the wilds of Canada, of course), mercifully seeing nobody.

In the meantime, our gamble had paid off. With dire threats of reprisals and punishments, in which the names of various parents were invoked, and with much shaking of the horse-whip, Ikey had departed down Ten Acre Reach to salvage his lighter. We went upstream in the opposite direction. It wasn't our side of the river, and the going was rough and tough, especially for Eric and me. We had to be helped quite a bit, all the time with a fearful feeling that we might be surprised by Farmer Ives. Eventually we reached the Four Poplars, stripped off our clothes, tied them into bundles, fastened them to the tops of our heads and swam across the river to safety.

How we laughed and congratulated each other on the success of our stratagems. Other boys who had been swimming at the Bay heard our story and were as amused as we were.

However, the mills of God grind slowly…

Later that evening, when Ray and I were having our supper there was a knock at the back door which Dadda answered. There stood Ikey Tooley, horsewhip, invective and all. We cringed. Dadda came in to fetch us out to apologise, which we did. Ikey breathed threats of prosecution for trespass, stealing of a lighter and damage caused. Dadda having made us apologise, humble pie burned the insides of our mouths like disinfectant. He gave Ikey a glass of ale and eventually Ikey departed, threatening that next time he caught us on his property, he would report us (a) to the police and (b) to the Squire, and the birching we would get would be far worse than the horsewhip.

Then came the reckoning. We were taken into the study, where Dadda gave us a verbal beating up, followed by the cane on our hands. We went to bed tearfully, but I'm afraid not in a state of grace. We considered, as we sucked our sore hands, that Ikey was a poor sport. We would have been prepared to take his medicine, but it was a lowdown trick to tell our parents. One of the moans we always had was that Dadda would insist that he was the headmaster of the village and that his children should be examples to the rest of the community and not the ringleaders of petty criminality. A hard row to hoe, but it was ever present with us.

I ought to add here that Dadda was marvellous where affairs of this sort were concerned. He would always settle any sort of hash. Even the local constable brought cases of delinquency to him, and Dadda, with the full cooperation of the parents, would always square matters off, to everybody's satisfaction. We never had any juvenile delinquency in our own village. Dadda had the measure of the village and of all its children. Parents trusted him and his justice.

But in telling you of the escapade, which I must say I look back on with a deal of amusement, I am forgetting the real subject matter of this chapter, the Caen Meadow. Of course, what made the Meadow so attractive to us was that glorious river, the Bure, which bounded the field on the western side. The river was a never-failing magnet to us. Why some of us were never drowned I just can't think. Perhaps it was because we could swim almost as soon as we could walk. Water had no terrors for us. Not so with Mumma; she dreaded it. As I have remarked before, she would regale us with horrifying stories of schoolgirl contemporaries of hers during her girlhood in Yorkshire who had been drowned, despite being good swimmers, on Sunday School picnics. She would warn us of the terrors of cramp and all the rest of it.

We were never allowed to swim on a Sunday. Along with adultery, swimming on the Sabbath was a sin that would not forgiven by the Holy Spirit. I can remember baking-hot Sunday afternoons when we would be lolling in the sun on the upper slopes of the Caen Meadow, hearing the splashes and happy cries of the bathers down at the Bay, yet we were forbidden on pain almost of excommunication, to go anywhere near the water.

The Bay was so called because at one time or another there must have been some sort of boathouse there. The remains of it could be seen if one took the trouble to look, but nobody I have ever spoken to could remember seeing a boathouse. When I walked into Wroxham School a year or so ago and mentioned the Bay to the older children, they had no idea where it was. They looked at me in blank amazement when I asked them if they still bathed there. The Headmaster hurriedly put in that because of the pollution in the river from chemicals and the sewage from pleasure craft, the children were told not to bathe in the river at all. I could have wept. In our day the schoolchildren bathed there after school, then the older boys and men as they came home from work, and the river water was crystal clear. Sic transit!

I can clearly remember the first time I swam there, or at least tried to. It was, if my memory is not deceiving me, in July 1911. It was a glorious sunny Saturday afternoon and Dadda and Mumma were out on their weekly shopping excursion to Norwich. All the boys were in and out of the water down at the Bay.   I envied my brother Ray and all the other boys and longed for a dip, but I had no bathing drawers, and we were meticulously careful about the proprieties.

I was on the verge of tears, and went up home to beg help from my sisters. Vicky took pity on me and fixed me up with a pair of her own navy blue knickers. I was delighted, and romped down the hill with my towel, telling everybody my problem had been solved. How the rest of the boys laughed! But never mind, tutored by the other boys and by my brother Ray, I was introduced to the cooling waters. I can still remember the coldness of the river water creeping up my little legs as I was led down into the river. The bottom shelved at that point rather like a beach at the seaside. The water reached my tummy, and then I drew an involuntary breath and took the plunge.

Supported by the other boys, I tried my first tentative swimming strokes.

By the end of that summer I had managed 'across the river' to the Four Poplars, and the river received me as a devotee from thenceforth.

CHAPTER SIX

The village school

It is difficult to know where to start when telling of my school. It is bound up so intimately with the formative years of my life that just to open a crack in the doorway of the memory is to summon a crowd of faces, of voices, of incidents, of laughter and sorrow, of joy and sadness.

When I visited the school a month or so ago, for the first time in some 40 years, I made for the spot which was the focus of my first recollection of it. It was just inside the door of what was known as the New Room, where it opened from the infants' lobby and the backyard of the school and the school house buildings. I have a distinct memory of an escape from whoever was in charge of me – I couldn't have been more than two or three at the most – and I remember that I was dressed in a little skirt. So far I hadn't progressed to 'breeks'.

I had made for this door and, after a little struggle, had opened it, to the huge delight of the 'big boys' who occupied a desk just inside the room. These boys were all great friends of mine. There were Horace, Henry, George, Duke and my own big brother Stanley, among many others. A forest of hands went up and there was a general cry of 'Sir, Sir, here's young Cliffy!"

I added to the din with a loud call of "I want my Dadda!" and Dadda rose from his desk, where he had been correcting an exercise with one of the boys standing by him. I tottered over to him, holding out my arms. I was lifted up, kissed and then told I must go back to Maria, or whoever was in charge of me, whereupon I was gently taken to the door through which I had entered.

Then I began to cry. Now I had found my Dadda, I didn't want to lose him again. The big boys took pity on me and asked 'Sir' if I couldn't stay with them. They would look after me. I think it must have been late in the afternoon, and the work of the day was beginning to tail off. Anyway Dadda let me go with them, so there I was having a marvellous time, being passed from desk to desk and from knee to knee. The 'big girls' dearly wanted me to go to them, but I preferred the boys, and with them I stayed until school was dismissed. How they spoiled me.

I suppose, too, that from that incident comes another fragrant recollection, that of prayers for the closing of the day's school. Dadda would open the partition door between the two rooms, we would stand, and the order would come, 'Hands together, eyes closed', and then Dadda would intone a collect, always the same one at the close of day. I usually dislike the term 'favourite' applied to anything, but I must claim this particular collect as my favourite. It is that of the 7th Sunday after Trinity.

Lord of all power and might, who art the author and giver of all good things: graft in our hearts the love of thy name, increase in us true religion, nourish us with all goodness and of thy great mercy, keep us in the same; through Jesus. Chris our Lord. Amen.

The collect would be intoned and we would sing 'amen' to it, and then after Grace had been said we would be dismissed, and in orderly fashion marched out of school. But all that is merely an introduction to the school.

It must have been shortly after this incident that I was admitted into the infant school, where Mumma was in charge. This had been built, I suppose, shortly after the Education Act of 1870, and was then, so far as I can ascertain, a one-room school. The buildings had been enlarged by the addition of another room, slightly larger, alongside the original room. About the turn of the century, shortly after Dadda had assumed the headship, a third room was added, known as the 'New Room'. The school buildings are of brick, ornamented with a special kind of moulded brickware peculiar to the Norwich district, called Costessy ware. This was made in the village of Costessy (pronounced Cossey) on the farther side of Norwich. I can remember how, in our early compositions describing the school, this ornamentation by Costessy ware was always a highlight. The schoolhouse windows and so on were similarly ornamented. They were pretty to look at, but the very devil for the glass-cutter should a broken window have to be replaced.

Compared with the primary schools of today, ours at Wroxham was very primitive. All 'loos' were, of course, outside and very unsanitary. I will spare you a description, but one usually waited until almost the last minute before putting up one's hand and asking permission to leave the room.

Inside the infants' room all was colour and light, and it was all very cosy. I can remember sand trays for the practice of lettering, and also, of course, for model-making and drawing. I used to enjoy making patterns with highly - coloured glossy strips of paper which one threaded through other vertical cut strips of another colour. And then there was 'ravelling'. Have you ever done any ravelling -, or should it be, have you ever ravelled? Let me tell you that it can either be a most soothing and restful employment to keep little ones quiet and their fingers occupied, or one of the most exasperating and nerve-racking engagements ever thought up by the perfidy of man.

The principle of the thing is this. Each member of the class is served out with a selection of pieces of material, say about 3" x 4" in size. These you set to work to tear to pieces – that is, you unravel them by pulling out the threads of which they are constructed. With pieces of loose-woven fabric such as tweed, all is peaceful and quiet and there is a sadistic satisfaction in the gradual destruction of the material to hand. But some pieces of material were originally woven by some black art, and these simply will not be unravelled no matter how you tug and strain. However hard you try, and no matter how sweaty and consequently how grubby these pieces of cloth become, they remain intransigent. They will not be overcome.

It was always laid down that your ravelling had to be completed by the end of the period. If incomplete, you might have to forgo playtime in order to catch up. It was an occupation I loathed. Many a tear have I shed over those pieces of cloth that would not be torn asunder - and what was the point of the exercise? Possibly to encourage patience, or mayhap perseverance. I have a sneaking idea that it was none of those things, but rather a supply line of 'fillings' for cushions and pillows to be hemmed and embroidered in needlework in the upper classes.

Still, for all that, we were a contented and placid little community, presided over by Mumma, who stood no nonsense. Here we learned our simple Bible stories. My knowledge of the stories of the Patriarchs in the Old Testament stem from those very early scripture lessons, with our primitive crayon drawings of the imagined scenes to round the lesson off. We sang choruses from a brown music book with gilded lettering on the outside, plus embossed 'Golden Bells'. A great favourite was one which started with the words, 'When Mothers of Salem their children brought to Jesus...' It was years before I discovered that Salem was another version of Jerusalem, so in my imagination Salem became all manner of weird places. From time to time, in 'singing all together', we would sing this in our reedy little voices to the big children, to their huge delight. It always 'went down big', as they say of stage successes.

In the infant school we learned our letters, we said the alphabet, scribed our pothooks and hangers and, before we departed for Standard 1 in the 'big school', had the elementary rudiments of copper-plate handwriting and knew up to our three times table. It was warm, secure, cosy and happy. Rarely were there tears, except maybe at the beginning of the term when the 'babies' joined and had to endure that awful lesson of bearing with separation from home. Mumma was a most comfortable and comforting body and it wasn't long before the stranger felt at home. She usually had a 'pupil-teacher' as an underling. We were brought up to be very polite and to honour and obey our betters, and whenever a stranger or visitor came into the room, to stand and acknowledge their status. This was the rule throughout the whole school.

Progressing upwards through the school we pass through a doorway halfway down the south wall of the Infants' Room and so into the Middle Room, which, as its name implies, was between the Infants' Room and the

New Room. The Middle Room was the home of Standards 1, 2, 3 and 4. Each two standards shared a teacher. A curtain hung laterally across the centre of the room and, naturally, for there to be any sanity, there was a rule of silence. Communication by word of mouth between pupils was not encouraged, and we were never allowed to waste time during the hours of tuition.

The front wall of the room was covered with charts and tables, spelling and dates in history and so on, plus, perhaps, the words of some song we were learning, or perchance the verses of a hymn. The timetable was strictly adhered to, and between the various lesson periods – say between Arithmetic and English – while books were being collected up and books for the next lesson distributed by monitors, another of the monitors would conduct us 'parrot-wise' through some table or other from the appropriate chart on the wall. It would be face towards us for, say, two recitals, and then turned away from us while we repeated it from memory so that our minds would be charged by this look-and-learn method.

Occasionally a teacher would break in, having had some lazybones under observation – and believe me, they knew all the slackers – and said the offending child would have to do a solo; that is, he or she would have to stand up and do a repetition inevitably to be caught out, of course, with the penalty of staying in at playtime to write the table out on a piece of paper. There are those who say that such 'parrot' methods are not only out of date but actually harmful. I am no child psychologist - I can only speak for myself and for the general level of scholarship in our school, which was high - but I am eternally grateful to the system, which grounded us in the 'three Rs' and gave us the basic facts upon which to rear, later on, our own contribution to the general structure of society. I know, too, that there are many teachers today who, although trained in modern educational methods, yearn for the old days when memory was not despised and children were 'taught'. But I digress.

We started the day with Scripture and this was always, in every class, followed by Arithmetic. Personally I loathed the latter, not having a brain attuned to mathematics, but arithmetic was taught not so much as the possession of a knowledge of numbers, but as a basic training in integrity and truthfulness. The correct answer to a sum set was an acknowledgement of the truth.

Dadda used to walk round his school to see how things were going at various times during the day, but particularly during arithmetic. He would arrive in front of the class and then, after a word to the teacher, would tell us to put our pens down, fold our arms and be prepared for about five minutes of mental arithmetic, to sharpen our wits and keep us alert. I was never any good at this and used to dread the sessions.

He would say, 'Add...' and there would follow a succession of numbers fairly quickly, until he would say, 'What is the answer?' and a forest of hands would go up. Those who were good at it would wave their hands wildly, hissing like a snake-pit in their eagerness to answer. 'Sir! Sir! Sir! they would sibilate. We dull-witted ones, not to be outdone, would feebly raise our hands and hope that our lame contribution to the exercise would not be called upon, but, true teacher that he was, Dadda would instinctively identify the waverer. He would be called upon to furnish an answer, and, having lost the gist of the whole thing after, say, the first three or four numbers, would be forced to justify having had his hand up to make some wild guess, to the huge delight of the quick-witted, who would be permitted a polite laugh at the expense of the victim. Dadda would then patiently go through the exercise again, teaching how one should add mentally without making mistakes, and we would try again. He would pass on to the next class to repeat the brain-teasers and to stimulate our mental processes. He was a great man, my father, and a wonderful teacher.

It was while I was in standards 3 and 4 that I remember being enlightened to an appreciation of the beauty of the English tongue. Dadda and Mumma were North Country folk who spoke with the slight brogue of the educated Yorkshireman. I and my contemporaries, up to the age of about seven or eight, spoke broad Norfolk, a lazy lilting dialect with its attractive local vocabulary and vowel sounds. Some say it is the nearest to the true English pronunciation. Be that as it may, consonants get short shrift from your true East Anglian.

A new teacher arrived at the school, fresh from college. Her name was Miss Fisher. She spoke beautifully and was determined to persuade as many of us as possible to smarten up our speech. She read beautifully and introduced us, commensurate with our years, to the cream of English literature. She exhorted us to speak carefully, quietly and with due respect for our native language, the language of the Bible and Shakespeare, as she told us. I can hear her now patiently teaching us to repeat 'Do not mutter, bread and butter', a rare trap for the East Anglian who makes that, 'Du no' muh'ah, bre' an' buh'ah'. Miss Fisher taught us to speak our language with a careful appreciation of its worth.

I remember too that our class readers at that time were *Masterman Ready* by Marryat, Ballantyne's *Coral Island* and Dean Farrar's mawkish story Eric, or *Little by Little*. Arthur's deathbed brought tears to our eyes, although we considered him a bit of a prig. *Masterman Ready* and *Coral Island* we loved. Their adventures served us with wonderful foundations for our games 'down the sloes' and across the Caen Meadow.

A moveable partition, which was always breaking down and coming off its rails, separated the Middle Room from what we called the New Room, i.e. the last to be built on to the school complex. This room accommodated standards 5, 6 and 7 and was where Dadda held sway. Here was his desk: the walls of the room were lined with cupboards in which were stored the stocks of school books and impedimenta for the pursuit of education. Here dwelt the wisdom of the establishment, the big boys and girls. Standard 5 was the age group from which came scholarship material, and it was presided over by yet another teacher, who was usually, unofficially, the Deputy Head. There always seemed to be an air of deep concentration and study in this room. A faint but subdued hum emanated from the pupils; not the mutter, mutter which would come from a chattering in subdued voices to one another – such a thing was unheard of – but rather a sub-audible self-to-self conversation concerning the matter of the study in hand. I am reminded of the psalmist's telling phrase, 'Deep calleth unto deep', such was the hum in the New Room.

From time to time this hum would increase, usually when the classes were involved in some extra mental effort; say arithmetic time, or wrestling with a composition (note we never called them essays). When the hum had become noticeably audible, Dadda would call 'Silence!' and the hum would turn off like the sudden cut-out of an electric motor. Usually, within five minutes or so, it would start up again, very quietly, and increase until there was another call for silence.

Corporal punishment was administered with a cane across the hand, and these solemn occasions were always enacted before Dadda's desk. A short lecture would precede the operation, together with a careful record of the occasion plus the number of strokes to be entered in the Punishment Book, always, if I remember rightly, carefully examined and initialled by the school managers when they called.

I think any of us would have chosen a caning rather than one of Dadda's lectures. He was one of those teachers who regarded the welfare of his pupils in all ways his responsibility and, without the unforgivable weapons of sarcasm, of rank unkindness or coldness, would make us fully aware of our shortcomings. Canings were rare, and only a last resort: a sort of shock treatment, never resented. We knew we deserved the punishment we got. Although we were the headmaster's children, our fellow pupils were honest with us and never regarded us as tell-tales. They would say exactly what they thought, and never did I hear any of them, at any time, complain about Dadda's justice and his administration of it – nor in the village today, amongst those of my contemporaries who survive, will one ever hear anything but affectionate remembrances of 'the Master'.

In comparison with the cosseting of school children today, our existence at Wroxham was bleak and hard, although I am certain that none of us was any the worse for it. The reputation of the school was such that children came from great distances and in all weathers to attend, and the percentages of attendance were very high, winter and summer alike. The Lodd family, for instance, came from Broad Farm, all of two miles away, the first part of it a long stretch of rough farm track before it joined the lane leading to Wroxham. The track would be almost impassable with mud in the winter, yet they always made it.

Still further were the cottages in a little hamlet called Bear's Wood. In my childhood, I was always convinced that bears did indeed dwell there and, although bluebells in season grew there in profusion, I was never all that keen on joining any expedition to pick them. Bear's Wood children must have had almost three miles to walk in all weathers. They usually came along a muddy footpath alongside the main railway line until they joined our main road. The Spurgeons, when they lived there, came from the outer lodge of Wroxham Hall, again a fair three miles along the main road. The keepers' children from the inner lodges would add another three quarters of a mile to that. The Shaxtons from the Hall Home Farm would come about two miles across the fields, muddy, exposed to all the winds that blew, and lonely.

There were, of course, no meals supplied in those days. The children brought sandwiches or what-have-you with them. In the winter they would cluster round the fire to eat their meal. On summer days maybe they would picnic on the Caen Meadow. There was a large contingent who came from beyond Wroxham Bridge, down towards Hoveton St John. They never grumbled or complained, nor did their parents.

I am trying hard to remember casualties at the school. I think that during the 12 years when I was actively connected with it, as a pupil first and a constant visitor after, I can only remember two deaths; a boy called Boyce who died under anaesthetic during an operation on his nose, and a boy called Francis Crane, known to us as Curly, who died after a long illness which must have been a type of leukaemia. The rest of us had our upsets, our fevers and our measles, but we weathered them all, and taking it by and large, were a very healthy crew.

The schoolrooms, even in the coldest weather, were always warm and welcoming. The good ladies from the village who cleaned saw to it that in winter the large fires, one in each room, were lit at an early hour. By the time the children started to straggle in from their long walks, the fires were burning brightly halfway up the chimney, and an adequate supply of coal was to hand in buckets alongside. Teachers and pupils saw to it that these fires never died down; perhaps for the last half hour of the day they would be allowed to sink into an honoured quietude of glowing embers.

On cold frosty mornings, as the children arrived in groups from their homes, they would be allowed in to thaw off in front of the fire. Wet boots and socks would be put to dry and Mumma and the other teachers would see to it that the children did not sit in class in damp clothes. Some children would bring slippers to change into, but our village families were not affluent enough to be able to supply such luxuries.

The school bell, rung by one of the crankiest pieces of mechanism I have ever struck, would ring a quarter of an hour before school started, warning any laggards that time was creeping on, and then it would ring again for us as a signal to assemble in our respective playgrounds, boys' and girls', each class in a line. On the order, we would march into school in military fashion, tidily and in step. More often than not, the first ones in would be started off by Dadda to sing the others into school, and they would join in as they came into the rooms. We were great singers at Wroxham and it was grand to see the big boys and girls marching in, heads held high to the martial strains of *See The Conquering Hero Comes, Men of Harlech, Hearts of Oak, The Minstrel Boy*, and many other such.

When all were in place we would stand for prayers which Dadda would take, standing in the doorway between the New and Middle Rooms. Prayers always started with a hymn with Mumma at the piano. We had a large repertoire of hymns and loved singing them. We would repeat the Lord's Prayer and Dadda would say a collect, usually that of the week. We would then sit while he made any announcements, after which the partition door would be closed, the registers called and the first lesson of the day, Scripture, would start.

I remarked above that we were a great singing school. Dadda had the great and rare gift of training children's voices, and I doubt whether there were any other schools that could have boasted such musical prowess. A School Inspector, Mr Key, would visit us periodically, and after walking round the school he would always ask to be entertained by our singing.

Dadda had been a chorister from his early years at Attercliffe Parish Church in Sheffield, where the standard must have been very high. There he must have learned and developed his genius for getting children to love singing. He believed, as I do, that once a boy has discovered the exquisite noise he can make by the proper control of his breathing, his vocal cords and his ears, you will never stop him singing until his voice breaks, and even then he will never lose his delight in singing.

This love of singing is catching. For the first week or so after a child arrived at Wroxham school he would attempt, in his own way, to join with us. Usually he would sing harshly in his chest voice, find himself unable to join us in our top Gs and As and wonder what he was doing wrong. Gently, kindly and persuasively Dadda, aided by the voices and the enthusiasm of the rest of us, would teach him how to produce his voice – how to sing – and in another few days he was caught forever as a singer.

We sang every day, and loved it. We had books of songs with staff notation, which we could read almost as fluently as our ordinary reading books. From the infant school all of us were taught to read staff notation. I can't remember a time when I couldn't read music. Teachers and educationalists could well follow Dadda's methods. You know those dull days in school, when it is heavy and rainy outside and an utter depression seems to descend on all? We had those days at Wroxham too, but Dadda would never admit defeat. It would be, "Put your pens down. Stand up. Breathe in – out – in- out. Now what shall we sing?" A chorus of voices would call for a variety of songs – as I said, our repertoire was enormous. A song would be chosen, Dadda would give us our note and off we would go. Perhaps we would sing songs, rounds or catches for 10 minutes or so and then Dadda would say "All right, that will do. Sit down and get on with your work". Invigorated, pepped up and happy, we would tackle our studies with renewed zest and joy of living.

'Singing all together' was a great treat. There was no regularity about this feast. Dadda would suddenly decide, before morning school started, that we would have what you might call today a 'sing-in'. As we played in the playground we would hear the older boys called into school and then hear the partition rumble back on its crazy lines, opening up New and Middle Rooms together. Then the cry would go round the playgrounds: "Singing all together!", and we couldn't wait to get into school to do it.

I am not speaking just of myself and my own enthusiasms but of us all. We loved it. Dadda would conduct the singing. Mumma would play the piano. We would start with our Morning Prayers preceded by a hymn or two, then would come our songs. The top school would sing their favourites, or perhaps the newest ballad they had learned – we always had one on the stocks. The middle school would offer their token of music. Catches, rounds and the like would be the amusement of the whole school – *Great Tom is cast, Hark the bonny Christchurch bells, Would you know my Celia's charms* and such morsels would be our delight. On occasion the infants would be brought in to sing such songs as:

A black cat walked in school one day,
Sh! Sh! Go out black cat...
or
Ding dong his hammer falls,
And the sparks fly up the walls...

We were quite sure these words referred to Mr Stevenson, the blacksmith. They were of course performed with appropriate hand, feet and head actions, which would convulse the upper classes and furnish us with huge enjoyment.

They were wonderful sing-songs. At the risk of boring you with my enthusiasm, I would love to give you a list of the songs we knew, which I can sing now, words and all, after all these years, but it would take up too much space. I do remember one ballad we were particularly fond of, which seems, looking back, to have been a strange choice: I remember needing it once in Hong Kong as an illustration for a broadcast programme and I had to record it myself or go without. The song was *The Death of Nelson*, a sentimental and patriotic ballad full of Victorian glucose. I have no idea now who wrote it, but we loved it and revelled in its sentiments. We lapped it up and saw ourselves as those hearts-of-oak (another of our favourites) who were Nelson's 'Band of Brothers'.

We had, at Wroxham, our regular seasons of enthusiasms. I can only call these outbreaks by such a name. They would appear almost overnight. It seems an age since I last saw a boy, or a girl, for that matter, spinning a top. One would go home from school, with no other thought in one's mind than, say, a game of 'toughing-out-of-home' down the sloes, or perhaps a bathe down at the Bay, but, hey presto, the following morning, as if by some strange juvenile telepathy, the tops would appear – not just one top or two, but a veritable army of them, some plain, some coloured, some squat and swarthy-looking, others tall and narrow. There would be whips to match and before one could say, 'John Barleycorn', the playground at the school would be full of top-spinning experts plying their art with vigour and determination, each spinner surrounded by an admiring galaxy of small boys, envying the operator, or maybe going to some quiet corner of the playground to try out their own puny skills.

Where did the tops come from, you ask? Well now, you have placed a poser. Since the majority of them were home-made, with a hobnail driven in at the spinning base to lessen friction, one should suspect a tradition of top-making, or maybe a cache of tops laid by in some peaceful corner of a house or back shed waiting for the top season to come round in order that they might be resurrected. In this way, some, you may be sure, were heirlooms passed on by older brothers.

There were, I remember, marvellous variations in the art of top-spinning.

For instance, one spinner would possess the skill, by dextrous manipulation of his whip, to be able to jump his top quite high in the air. I can remember Lenny Brown, a great top spinner, spinning his top up a shallow flight of stone steps and down again.

The craze would last, say, a week or a fortnight, and then, as suddenly as the tops had appeared, they would vanish again. After a short quietude when we would revert to football or high-cockalorum or something like that, one morning, hoops would be bowled into the playground. There would be tall hoops, made of wrought iron with cunningly devised iron crooks, pretty pieces of ironmongery, to bowl them. These were circles of varying diameters made by Mr Stevenson, our blacksmith, who always found time to produce such toys for those needing them. Other hoops were spokeless bicycle wheels. A smooth stick cunningly applied in the 'v' shape where formerly the tyre had been housed, suitably greased, made a wonderful machine, capable of being driven at high speeds. They were very manoeuvrable. Hoops, of course, were a winter pastime. since the exercise they needed to keep them in motion kept us as warm as toast in our biting east coast winds.

Summertime introduced marbles. One could buy highly-coloured marbles at Oliphants or Bresciani's, our local village stores – where, incidentally, everything could be purchased and where the storekeepers seemed strangely to be in tune with our telepathic adoption of the current craze. But the best marbles were those which had belonged to Granddad and had been in the family for more years than one could reckon. The ones from the shop were not frightfully strong, and, although attractive to look at, they were made of hard-baked clay, whereas those resurrected from the family store were small and literally 'marble' or perhaps hard pebble. These were unbreakable and, moreover, the bouncing power, if I can call it that, supplied by their weight, made them sure winners.

This was particularly so in our favourite marble game, that of bouncing your marble against a wall with the objective of landing it close enough to that of your adversary to allow you to span your fingers from one to the other, thus collecting both. There were alley taws too, big glass marbles with wonderful streaks of colour inside them. These were mainly used for games on the flat, the 'ring' game (sometimes seen being played by experts in Yorkshire on TV). A circle is roughly drawn with the finger in the dust on level ground. A number of marbles were placed inside the ring by the various players. The game was to flick your marble from outside the circle to knock one or more of your opponents' marbles out of the circle. These marbles became your winnings.

A variation of this was a progressive game, played along the gutters to and from school, in which you flicked your marble ahead of you, hoping to 'span' and win that of an opponent. Many were the variations, and year by year the old 'tried' real marbles would reappear, the most devastating winners being known as 'dimshies'. I often wonder where, in this modern and sophisticated world, one would be able to find such earnest games of marbles of so many varieties being played with such absorption.

Skipping ropes had a short, concentrated season, and were used mostly by the girls. We boys always looked upon them as beneath our notice. We used them only if some challenge were put, when we would rally to the defence of our prowess at anything.

But I cannot bring this section of my saga to an end without a mention of popguns. They were a late summer activity, and I cannot ever recall seeing them made and used in any locality other than ours. I'm probably talking through my hat here, but I can honestly say that I have never seen or heard of them outside Wroxham.

A popgun was made from a straight piece of elder wood with the pith at the centre carefully gouged out, usually with the aid of a red-hot piece of iron wire. Then a straight piece of seasoned hardwood, scrounged from a local carpenter, would carefully be whittled down until its diameter was almost the width of the pith-hole left in the elder wood barrel. This piece of wood, carefully rounded and trued, would have a handle left at one end. The other end would be 'towed', that is, moistened by one's spit and hammered against the nearest hard surface, say a brick wall, until it was tow-headed, in other words until it looked rather like a diminutive mop head. This piece of wood, tow-headed at one end and with a handle at the other, would become the ramrod - except that it was for firing the gun, not loading it. The tow-head was, of course, to form an air seal.

Having done all this to the successful conclusion of your skill, you then proceeded to try it out by loading it. You took an acorn whose circumference was slightly larger than that of the barrel of your popgun, bit it in half and hammered one half, curved end inwards of course, into one end of the barrel and the other half similarly into the other. This was usually done against a wall, which, of course, stained the wall as the juice of the acorn dried. Biting the acorns always produced soreness round the mouth, which wasn't popular with parents.

To fire the popgun, you nestled the handle end of the ramrod in your tummy and forced the tow-end into one of the acorn-filled ends of the barrel. As the pressure inside the barrel increased, the opposite half of the acorn would be shot out with a loud and satisfactory pop. The better the gun was constructed, the louder and better the pop.

We never used these guns to fire at each other, but rather to see how accurately and how far we could shoot a half acorn. Popguns could, of course, be stored through the winter, but this wasn't very successful. It was more usual to make them afresh every year. Some were beautifully constructed with carving on the outsides and were the pride of their makers. They could be short, long, fat or thin, according to the whim of the maker, but everybody had to have one.

Eventually, as winter advanced and the acorns disappeared, so would the popguns. Dadda would complain of the stains on the school walls caused by the hammering-in of the acorns, and we would have to spend a playtime scrubbing them off. All the same it was great fun, and certainly the longest-lasting and most popular of our seasonal crazes.

In the spring we made whistles from the newly-grown willow wands, and very successful they were. It was a short season and the whistles could be made only when the sap was rising and it was possible to peel the green bark off the saplings without cracking them.

Bows and arrows came in for a short season. These were home-made from ash saplings, with strong cord bowstrings. The arrows were made from thatching reeds pulled from the roof of Farmer Haylett's barn, just down the road from the school. A length of reed to match the size of your bow would be chosen. A 'cot' or head was made from a piece of elder wood about three inches long and the reed would be pushed into its pith centre. At the other end a small 'v' would be cut into the arrow, and there was your weapon. They could be dangerous, and we were always being warned about this. One of the Haines boys lost the sight of an eye through being accidentally hit by an arrow. We had nicknames for everyone, so he at once became known as Nelson.

One could go on and on with the seasons of this and that. They lasted us well through the year, and none were ever omitted. There was the collection of 'fag cards' (from packets of cigarettes in those days), and the games that went with them. There were 'peep-shows' – the inside of a shoebox would be fitted at one end with a cut-out scene, and the lid would have a circle cut out of it and the hole covered with coloured tissue paper. A peep-hole would be cut in the end opposite the scene and customers would be charged one fag card per peep. Some of these peep-shows, I remember, were strangely beautiful, and the manufacture of them was much encouraged by the teachers.

I cannot close this section without a mention of Empire Day, now alas gone. We looked forward to it and practised for it, and on the great day, we would form up in the playground after prayers. While we sang the National Anthem and *God Bless the Prince of Wales*, the Union Flag would solemnly be hoisted by one of the monitors and we would march round in our classes saluting the flag which flew bravely on its tall flagpole. We would return into school to sing many of our patriotic songs, of which we had a large repertoire, while our teachers would talk of the Empire with the aid of a large wall map, making us swell with pride in our national heritage.

Then there was Mayday, with its songs and dances in the playground – the girls in their pretty frocks, the senior ones dancing their Morris dances with the boys.

Woe betide the luckless wight who couldn't find an oak apple on Oak Apple Day. He would be chased with nettles as an anti-Royalist, and the pursuit would not be called off until he had been well stung – little savages we were at times. If there was a scarcity of oak apples, some of us had a rough time of it with the nettles.

What a happy and contented community we were at Wroxham School. We were never at a loss for something to do, never bored, always singing, deeply fond of our school and our teachers and tremendously proud of our unique village and our country.

CHAPTER SEVEN

Rights of way

Somewhere about the turn of the century (I suppose I could look up the exact date, but it doesn't matter overmuch), there had been a lawsuit in the village over the question of a right of way. We were a great community for Sunday afternoon walks, and a favourite stroll was that which led 'across the fields'. This was a footpath, at times widening into a cart track, which stretched between Wroxham and a remote little village called Crostwick. I haven't been there for more years than I care to count, but I must see Crostwick again some time, if only for old time's sake.

The footpath was unfenced most of the way and it would wind through woods and fields, rich with blackberries, sweet chestnuts, wild strawberries or the occasional field mushroom, all according to season. There was plenty of fresh air and lots of room. You know how children and dogs always cover at least double the ground of their elders by exploring the immediate surroundings of the set track? So it was with the footpath to Crostwick.

Unfortunately the track marched through the preserves of the 'Old Squire', as we called him, and villagers on their walks, attended by their children and their skirmishes, plus the occasional dog, could play havoc. The potential damage to hedges and gates, along with the possible scaring of game and so on, was anathema to him. He was very jealous of his property and waged a constant war against trespassers of all kinds.

This episode took place a few years before I appeared on the scene, so I am only going on hearsay culled many years ago. One Sunday afternoon the village walkers set off for their customary favourite stroll only to find gates erected and gamekeepers standing by them, turning back all and sundry and stating that in future the footpath could not be used. People needing to go to Crostwick could go round by the proper road. 'Across the fields' was not a right of way, and would they please mark that for future reference.

That Sunday night, the ancients of the village went up in smoke. In the Castle Inn, a real old-fashioned thatched village pub in those days (unfortunately later to be destroyed by fire), heads were shaken and plans were laid to thwart the Squire and his-ill laid schemes of enclosure - for that is what they assumed it was. So far as I can gather, nobody dared to challenge the Squire's edict in person by attempting to pass the barriers, but lawyers were approached, advice was taken and finally one day there was a grand exodus of the village fathers to London, where the case was to be heard.

To cut a long story short, the Squire lost the day. I am told that a number of people who had given evidence against the enclosure lost their jobs, and the Squire there and then, apart from absolute necessity, cut himself adrift from the village and its affairs. He wished to preserve his privacy. I can distinctly remember the warnings given by our elders never to stray into the Squire's woods nor scare his pheasants.

To the best of my knowledge and recollection I never set eyes on the man, but I can clearly remember his funeral. The 'Squirearchy' were Roman Catholics, devout ones, but they have a large burial mausoleum in the churchyard of the village church. The funeral procession was to come down Church Lane past our house en route to the Church. It was a dreadful afternoon. There was a tremendous thunderstorm with torrents of rain and the usual wild winds that accompany such tempests. The Squire's hearse was a decorated farm wagon drawn by shire horses from the estate farms. The mourners were, of course, in horse-drawn coaches but the local Scout troop, newly formed, marched all three miles or so from the hall alongside the wagon. The estate workers also walked as pall bearers, all soaked to the skin.

My brother and I were invited to go to Holly Lodge, the blacksmith's house just across the Caen Meadow, where, from the shelter of Mrs Stevenson's wash kitchen, we would be able to get a better view of the proceedings. We could see the road and most of the churchyard from our vantage point. I remember that my sister Vicky and Winnie Stevenson, her bosom friend, watched from under the shelter of some pollarded lime trees, which bordered the road down which the cortège was to come.

The rain fell in torrents and lightning crackled and split the atmosphere with frightening peals of thunder, which reverberated across the valley and the marshes. As the procession slowly passed Holly Lodge, Mr Stevenson, an old Indian Army man, fired blanks over the coffin. It was all most impressive to us small fry, who had never seen such goings-on in our village before. We saw the wagon and the coaches arrive at the gate of the churchyard and the coffin being lifted from the hearse. Then we saw the choristers and acolytes from the Roman Catholic Cathedral in Norwich, together with their priests, get out of their carriages and form their procession with a smoking censer, escorting the coffin of the Old Squire in the blinding rain to its last home.

We wished that we had been allowed nearer, rain or no rain, thunder or no thunder, to gape at the Catholic Norwichers and maybe to get a sniff of the incense, which we had never sampled before, but this was not allowed. We stayed in Mrs Stevenson's wash kitchen till all the excitement was over, the thunder had ceased and the rain had set in, steely and straight. From our shelter we watched the drenched ecclesiastics and mourners leave our churchyard and return the three miles or so across the fields back to the Hall. Some of the elders who had been active during the lawsuit saw in the thunder and lightning and the general disturbance a judgement on the Old Squire. We pronounced on such things in that way and believed in our pronouncements.

The Old Squire gone and his attempts at closures foiled, we were free to walk 'across the fields'. It was our favourite walk. On Sunday afternoons, our parents usually enjoying a well-earned afternoon nap, we would set out clutching an orange or an apple. Up Church Lane we would go to the top of the hill. Here the lane wound left to the Castle Inn and the main road to Norwich, passing over the railway en route. To the right, the rough track we called Sot's Hole led down to a public staithe by the river. There were some cottages down by Sot's Hole, originally built to house the employees of a large malthouse which had once stood by the river, but they had long ago been pulled down. For our walk, we turned neither to the right nor the left but headed straight over the brow of the 'hill' - in any other county it would have been called a slight rise.

Anyway, over the hill we went, leaving Hill Farmhouse and its farm on our right. We were now in Skinner's Lane on our way to 'across-the-fields'. On the right beyond a high hedge were two fields of pastureland sloping gently down to the river. The second of these was a field which was sometimes rich in mushrooms in high summer. Many is the time I have set out in the early morning to glean some of this delicious fungus to be cooked for Dadda's breakfast.

Immediately beyond this point came the first of the gates which had been erected by the Squire. They had never been removed, a reminder perhaps that the Squire hadn't finished with us yet. A rutted lane led to another set of gates, to the right of which stood (it still stands) a gaunt redbrick house in unmistakeable Victorian architectural style. This was known as the Priest's House, and in it lived the private chaplain to the Hall folk. Why they should have built this house so far from the family seat – a good two or three miles – I can't think. There was a chapel at the Hall, and it was there that the services for the Roman Catholic household were held. There were no Roman Catholics to my knowledge living in the village. It seems so odd that this house, quite a pleasant one with a long garden reaching down to the river and with its own boathouse, should have been planted so far from the Priest's orbit of ministry.

At a later period of my boyhood, with the retirement of Canon Grogan, chaplain to the Hall for some years and a great friend of Dadda, the house was let to other people. The last chaplain I can remember, Father Hampson, lived in digs opposite the school with a highly respected Methodist family. He was a most interesting man and a great friend to the children of our area. He invented things; for instance he had a wonderful model of a paddle-boat tug, quite a large model, and he had taken the clockwork engine out of it and had replaced the motive power with some form of wind vane on the mast. This would turn in a moderate breeze and, by a cunning manipulation of gear wheels, the paddleboat would make steady progress along the river bordering the Caen Meadow. Whenever we saw the good priest with his boat we would rush along to him, eager to watch and learn.

Strangely enough, some many years after, a similar principle was applied to a merchant ship, I think sailing from Holland. The wind vanes had been replaced by a tall cylinder with a type of turbine blade fitted, but the underlying principle was the same. I can't recollect that it was ever successful commercially. Father Hampson also invented a type of long-distance rangefinder for gunnery (my memory is not very clear here as I couldn't understand it), consisting of a semi-circle of cardboard carefully marked out in degrees with a piece of string attached to the point halfway along the straight side. That is probably a very wrong description of the apparatus, but that is how I remember it. By pointing towards the object whose range was required, fiddling about with the piece of string and applying a simple mathematical rule of thumb, the range would rapidly be given.

Some of the other boys got enthusiastic over this and were very good at it, to the delight of Father Hampson, but mathematically-blind Clifford never made the grade. Father Hampson used to be driven to the Hall for his services and duties by our worthy Mr Stevenson in a dogcart drawn by a piebald pony called Tommy, and a very smart turnout it was too. That seems a long time ago.

I had better continue with our walk, or teatime will be over before we finish it. Emerging from the rutted lane through the gate and leaving the priest's house, we came to a broad footpath, very muddy in winter, which led across the Priest's Fields, taking their name of course from the house. The two fields, or rather I suppose it should be one field divided by the footpath, were to my boyish eyes a vast tract of open country.

I can clearly call to mind the ploughing of these fields on one occasion by a steam plough. Two enormous and powerful steam locomotives were positioned at opposite ends of the fields. Between them was stretched a long steel cable which hauled to and fro a huge primeval-looking machine with some eight to 10 ploughshares attached. Enormous drums under the engines, geared to the power unit, slowly revolved, either hauling in or paying off the steel rope as the monster plough advanced over the brown land, gashing it with deep scores eight to 10 at a time. After each double crossing of the field, both engines had to be moved along for the next ploy.

It was fascinating to watch. The plough itself was two-way; there were two sets of ploughshares, one taking its turn at ploughing, the other up in the air like the back fin of some primeval monster. The one in use would be winched up and the other let down at each turn round. As with the sighting device, I feel this description may not be as clear as it might have been, but I think you will see what I mean and appreciate how it all worked. Such machines are now museum pieces. I am grateful that I can remember seeing them earning their living in the heyday of the steam traction engine.

The path over the Priest's Fields was almost three quarters of a mile from one end to the other. It was broken halfway across by a solitary oak tree, warped and gnarled – it had no shelter from the winds that blow, and blow they did from all quarters of the compass. Reaching the end of this footpath and approaching another gate, we came to the first of the sweet chestnut woods. The trees were inside the fence, and knowing the Squire's touchiness about trespassers on his preserves we always had to plant a guard to warn of the approach of keepers - or of any strangers for that matter, as they might be keepers in disguise.

In the chestnut season, if there had been violent winds, the profusion of chestnuts on the ground would occupy us for the rest of our walking time and we would get no further. Still this only happened in late autumn, so we may safely continue on our walk.

The route led through another gate, through a small copse of oak trees and down a very muddy lane to some cottages on the right near a stile and gate. Here one came in sight of the Home Farm, still some considerable distance from the Hall. At the top of a little rise beyond the cottages one was faced with a choice of route, and the solution depended on what the weather had been like. If one took a sharp turn to the left through another gate there was now a short, straight roadway called Mire's Baulk. One could, after very wet weather, avoid the muddy tracks of the farm road skirting the Home Farm by taking Mire's Baulk over to a better road at the other end, thus safely baulking the mire.

Leaving that for a moment, we will take the road past Home Farm. There were some splendid chestnut trees just past the farm buildings. There were even more attractive ones along the road which, marked with a 'Trespassers will be prosecuted' sign, turned off to the right to form the tradesmen's way to the Hall. This was a Tom Tiddler's Ground, so close to the Hall stronghold that I can never remember any of us daring, chestnuts or no chestnuts, to venture on to it. We kept strictly to the trodden track along here. It was always possible that in this neighbourhood we might walk into the Squire himself (the son of the Old Squire) or one of his keepers, and although we were strictly within our rights on the road they could make us feel most uncomfortable by their questions and veiled suggestions that we were on dangerous ground and it would be better for us to turn back.

"Don't let me hear my pheasants calling" the Squire would say. "I know who you are and I'll know that you have been after nuts in my plantation." And we would mutter under our breaths, "Yes sir, no sir, three bags full sir" and bravely press on. The Squire would let us go with a half-smile, but the Head Keeper, a Mr Hagan, could be most unpleasant, hinting of mantraps to catch poachers and their dogs. We were brave; we never turned back, although there might well have been a score of the Squire's chestnuts burning holes in our pockets.

I can remember the Sunday afternoon in 1911 when I made my first conscious contact with the newly-formed Scout movement, about which more in another chapter. It was the time of the Coronation of George V. The Squire had decided to bury the hatchet with the village and had allowed part of his land near Mire's Baulk to be used as a sports arena in celebration of the Coronation. For the first time ever, the newly-formed Scout troop were in camp there. Dadda was the Scoutmaster. He must have been one of the first Scoutmasters, since the inspiration for the formation of the troop came from a retired Boer War veteran, a Colonel S F Charles of Wroxham House, who was a close friend of Sir Robert Baden Powell. We were therefore early off the ground in our scouting. I can remember Dadda striding about the place in a grey knickerbocker suit (which incidentally also did duty when he turned out with the local unit of the Red Cross), and of course his Scout hat. Dadda flatly refused to get into shorts and the rest of the scout get-up.

During the weekend we had run races, enjoyed a sumptuous tea and received a Coronation mug each. On this particular Sunday afternoon, when the campsite was open to visitors, the outstanding event for me was when Stanley, my older brother, got bitten on the cheek by a wasp which had settled on some bread and jam he was eating. Funny how one remembers things like that. It was a very hot day and I went into Stanley's tent, an old army bell tent, and lay down on his straw palliasse to see what it felt like. Just then, horror of horrors, an earwig fell off the tent canvas on to my face. I ran out of that tent as though the hounds of hell were chasing me. I have never like earwigs from that day, and I still don't trust them, although I remember reading somewhere or other that in the insect world they are known to be good mothers – whatever that may mean.

Leaving Mire's Baulk or the Home Farm buildings, depending on which route one took, we would come eventually to the main front gateway of the drive leading to the Hall. I have never passed those portals. I can remember the Squire of my day, Mr Sigismund Trafford, bringing home his bride. We walked up from the village and stood waiting at the gates to the front drive for the bridal party to arrive. Flags and a triumphal arch of welcome had been erected by the estate workers and when the carriage appeared, how we cheered. I can remember to this day the radiant smile we got from the very pretty bride and how charming she looked. As we said in the village after,

"And she was a real lady too".

Incidentally, a memory slips in here of a walk once taken with Dadda past these gates and the lodge opposite, which was adorned, as were all the principal gates on the estate with the Trafford family crest, a man wielding a flail with the motto underneath reading, 'Now Thus'. We asked the meaning of it and Dadda told us that an ancestor of the Trafford family, a yeoman farmer, had been threshing his corn with a flail when either Charles I himself or one of his close friends, hotly pursued by Government troops, rushed into the barn and asked for help. The yeoman gave the King his smock and flail and hurriedly taught him how to swing it with the words 'Now thus'. When the soldiers arrived on the spot they found only two labourers wielding flails, and so the King escaped. Later the family were awarded the crest and its motto. That may or may not be a true rendering, but it was the one Dadda told us.

I remember some years after using it as an illustration to a sermon I was preaching in Truro Cathedral. One of the Canons remarked on the story and the crest and told me it was also to be found at the Old Trafford cricket ground in Manchester. Small world, isn't it?

All these digressions are lengthening this walk, so we'd better go on. Leaving the main gate on our right, we walked along a cart track with a long brick wall and a plantation of trees on our right and open fields on our left. This track led across further fields and some open scrubland to the village of Crostwick. It was a fairly straight path passing through some of the most fruitful and prolific blackberry bushes in our district. You can understand why we locals didn't want this right of way to be taken from us.

The scrubland which followed the field path was known locally as 'Fuzzbunt'. Dadda told us that it was really 'Furze Burnt', recalling possibly some ancient heath fire which had caused such a stir that its name had clung to the district, which was rich in furze bushes, a yellow glory in late spring. Here there were three or four labourers' cottages - they may still be there so far as I know, as I haven't been that way for a long time. Usually there would be children playing in the immediate neighbourhood, but on seeing us approach along this lonely footpath they would retreat to their gardens and hang over the gates or wall, thumbs in mouths, watching us dully without comment as we passed by.

If a mother happened to be in sight, she might look at us askance and call her children away from the gate, as though we might be the bearers of bubonic plague. We would slowly walk past, turning round off and on to see if they were still watching us, but never a word passed between us. Strange. Even at this moment of writing I can sense the silence and a kind of hostility about 'Fuzzbunt'. Perhaps it had been a stranger passing by who had set fire to the furze long long ago, and that memory had remained with them for all time – 'Never trust a stranger'.

I wonder where those children went to school. Our school at Wroxham was much too far for them, and there were no school buses in those days. Crostwick School was quite a distance too.

Two fields or so more, each with its stile or its kissing gate, and we came to a metalled road, the road to Crostwick. A few yards along this road we had reached the turning point of our walk, a stream flowing through a culvert under the road called Dobb's Beck. Please don't ask me why it had this name – I have no idea. Perhaps my writing this will cause me, or some other person, to look it up – not that it matters much, except for sentiment's sake.

This beck had a great fascination for us, since it actually bubbled over the stones like miniature rapids. This was such a rarity in Norfolk that always, on approaching it, we would stand in awe for a minute or so and watch the water bubbling along. We would talk about it to newcomers. 'Have you been to Dobb's Beck?' we would say, as though it was one of the wonders of the world. We would stop by the little bridge and play our own version of Poohsticks (although, of course, Pooh hadn't been thought of yet) and watch our little boats go under the bridge to emerge on the other side. Watercress grew there in profusion and we would gather some to take home with us.

The beck was a real wonder to us. Almost all our Norfolk streams were slow-flowing, so it was a great novelty. A visit paid to Dobb's Beck was a visit paid, shall we say, outside the county.

I remember one amusing episode concerning Dobb's Beck. Dadda had been reading Lorna Doone to us on our Friday afternoon sessions, and I distinctly remember his reading the passage concerning the boy John Ridd going to the river Lyn with a 'loach fork' to fish for loaches to take to his mother, who was out of sorts. You may remember how the writer describes in vivid detail the rushing Lyn and the loaches hiding under the stones. Stanley Stevenson, Eric's brother, always of an inventive turn of mind, decided that loaches must live in Dobb's Beck. On the Saturday that followed this reading he organised an expedition, taking a picnic lunch, to catch them. We made loach forks as per Lorna Doone and sallied forth to catch these delicacies. We took jam jars to hold the catch. Needless to say, none of us had the slightest idea what a loach looked like.

We arrived at Dobb's Beck in a state of great excitement, removed shoes and stockings and set to work to turn over stones, our loach forks at the ready. Naturally we saw nary a fish. Stanley, Eric, Ray and I would have caught all the loaches in the beck, had there been any. We had to satisfy ourselves with a jar full of tadpoles and some watercress. But the expedition had been well worthwhile. Our sisters laughed at us, Mumma was mildly amused (though she never looked with favour on anything to do with water and its incipient dangers), but Dadda commended our enterprise and, publicly in school the next Friday afternoon, congratulated us.

Beyond Dobb's Beck, a little way along the Crostwick Road, you could turn to the right, if you knew what you were doing, and go through a gate and along a deeply rutted lane with very high hedges to emerge on the 'safe side'. This was neutral ground, a bridge over a stream known locally as 'High-low Bridge'. It was built of brick, faced on either wall top with stone, and it conveyed you over a deepish gully with a stream, originally Dobb's Beck, at the bottom. The stream was slow and sluggish, meandering along between wooded banks which sloped steeply up and were covered with trees of all kinds, mostly conifers. The stream ultimately flowed into the Bure, only a short distance beyond the bridge.

It was always very, very quiet there. There were no farms or farm buildings anywhere in the neighbourhood. The roadway over the bridge led into enemy country, the domain of the Squire and his keepers. A little way beyond its far end it was joined by another, which led from the Hall. If one turned to the left the road descended, fairly steeply for Norfolk, to a staithe by the river's edge, known as Marl Staithe. There had once been an inn there, the haunt of wherrymen, but in our day there was only a forlorn-looking group of keepers' cottages. The inn had gone with the disappearance of the trading wherries which had called there for the loading of marl, used for the building and repair of roads. There must have been a marl pit in the immediate neighbourhood, although we never located it.

The inn, of course, would be to slake the thirst of the wherrymen. It was the most isolated spot. Apart from the overgrown clearing indicating that the place had at one time been occupied, there is now no sign of habitation there, not even a tumbledown shed.

In our day the cottages, as I have said, were occupied by keepers. Should we ever venture there by river or by land, daring to step over High-low Bridge into 'enemy territory', nobody ever challenged us. The same brood of non-communicative, staring children would watch us from a safe distance. They must have been related in some way to the 'Fuzzbunt' clan – their behaviour was so similar.

I remember once landing there by boat. A woman was taking water from the river in a bucket and we asked her if it would be all right to walk up the road to High-low Bridge. She turned away to walk to the house, leaving us standing hesitant on the river bank. As she entered the door of the house, having collected two children en route, she stared at us again and said in a hostile voice, "It's nothin' to do with me what you do". Then she slammed the door.

One never lingered there. It was an act of bravado even to set foot on that territory. It would have been terrible indeed to have walked into the Squire doing his rounds.

By the way, I had better explain the name – the bridge roadway was quite high over the stream, but the arch over the water was very low. You get the idea – Norfolk people are great ones for the exact descriptive phrase and the appropriate nickname for anybody and anything. When we visited it we always examined and commented upon the hundreds of initials which had been carved into the stone parapet. Generations of lovers had been attracted by the silence, the beauty and the loneliness of the spot, and had left their record behind.

My Uncle George, my mother's brother, had brought his fiancée down from Sheffield and they had added their initials. We always sought their names out when we visited the bridge – I could go there now and find them. I know exactly where they are.

The surrounds of the bridge were known as Little Switzerland. Nature had landscaped that forgotten little district into a picturesque terrain which had touched even we flat-earthed Norfolk dumplings with a rare eye for beauty. It was always so quiet, so still. We children never attempted to raise our voices there. We would be content to lean over the bridge and watch the slow-flowing stream with coloured water ferns on its surface, flag iris along its edge and the occasional white or yellow water lily. I saw my first ever kingfisher at High-low Bridge, a stroke of steely-blue lightning. What a thrill that was.

Once we used a particularly valiant ploy. Ray, the two Stevenson boys, and I walked to High-low Bridge, crossed it and then, instead of turning left down to Marl Staithe, we turned right and walked, without being challenged by anybody, right through the Hall grounds, past the back entrance to the Hall and down the back drive to the Home Farm. From there we could walk back to Wroxham across the fields. You have no idea what a brave thing that was for us to do. Mr Stevenson, in addition to being the village blacksmith, was blacksmith to the estate and had a forge near the Home Farm. Had the

Squire or any of his keepers caught us it wouldn't have just been a wigging from Dadda but ultimately trouble on the home front.

However, we were not caught. I certainly found out what it meant to carry one's heart in one's mouth, for every time we turned a corner or heard a footstep approaching we feared for our very lives. Several estate workers saw us, but presumed that since we were the sons of the schoolmaster and the blacksmith we must have had some sort of a right there and so didn't question us.

We boasted of that for many a long day. I wonder whether Stanley Stevenson or his brother Eric remembers it now.

Before I close this chapter of reminiscences of our wanderings round Wroxham I feel I must tell of another venture into the forbidden territory of 'rights of way'. Usually my brother Ray and I, Stanley and Eric Stevenson and Sidney Read, who were with us on the grand adventure with Ikey Tooley's fodder barge, were inseparable. We did everything together and had no secrets from one another. But one summer holidays, for some reason we could not fathom, Eric and I found that the older boys were giving us the slip. Search how we would, track and follow as we did with all the woodmanship at our command, we could not discover where they were going or what they were doing when they got there. When we asked them, they were evasive and gave no satisfactory answers. Eric and I were as mad as hornets over the whole affair.

Then it was that fate played into our hands. I cannot remember what particular wickedness it was, but Eric and I somehow got a hold over his brother Stanley. We discovered something that opened up the possibilities of blackmail. We told him that either he opened up as to what he and the other boys were doing and where they were going or we would tell his mother what he had been up to. Shabby and despicable I know, but they wouldn't play, and we didn't see why we should.

We put the whole thing to him, having got him on his own, but he was loyalty itself and refused to divulge anything until he had consulted the others.

This having been done, we were called into conference down in the bushes on the Caen Meadow and the matter was debated. They tried by bribery to buy us off, but we wouldn't play, so they had to take us into their confidence.

First, in the manner of Tom Sawyer, they swore us to secrecy. Then they told us to follow them. Across Stevensons' garden we went, over Chamberlain's meadow, under the bullus tree near the old Vicarage, across Church Meadow, until eventually we arrived in Sid Read's garden and into the forbidden territory of Ikey Tooley's marshes and alder carrs.

We had had our fracas with Ikey over the matter of the fodder barge not long before this, and Ikey had sworn summary vengeance on us of he caught us on his land again. One must give the older boys some credit here, because this was one of the reasons they gave us for not wanting us to be mixed up in the matter. However, after traversing the first patch of marsh with its small thickets or carrs of willow and alder, we came to a slightly thicker wood growing in very wet and muddy marsh, as if there might at one time have been a small land-locked broad there, in which these trees had taken root and established themselves. The only way of making safe progress through this wood was by exercising a sort of Tarzan swing through the boughs with the hope of finding firm landings for our feet on the marshy tussocks surrounding the boles of the trees where they emerged from the mud.

The older boys were very careful with us. They knew what trouble they would encounter if we smaller fry fell into the mud, so our progress through the wood was very slow.

After having gone some considerable distance, we were told to be very silent. A few more yards and we pushed through some thick clumps of reeds, some of them giant reed mace (ignorant folk call them bulrushes), to find ourselves standing on a little staithe of firm grass. In front of us, surrounded by trees festooned with hanging lichen and creepers, was a diminutive broad not more than a few yards across, with a little island in the centre on which grew a few ferns and a small bush of mountain ash scarlet with berries, and round the edges a yellow-green fringe of flag iris. There were water lilies both yellow and white there, together with their large green plate-like leaves floating on the water. The edges of this still pool were covered with the pale green and pink leaves of the water fern, as we called it.

After a short while, when all had quietened down after our arrival on the scene, a mother duck emerged from her hidey hole with a brood of furry ducklings. Birds whistled in the surrounding trees, a flight of bright pink jays exploded on to the mountain ash to sample its berries and we boys just stood silently and gaped at it all, still as the trees around. It was a lovely afternoon and we could look up through the lacy boughs of the trees overhead and see the clear blue of the sky which was reflected in the waters of the little lagoon. I think it was one of the most wonderful moments in my life. We boys and the creatures of the wild were in all probability the only ones who were privileged to enjoy this glory.

After half an hour or so we left. We were very silent in our going. None of us spoke a word except when it was absolutely necessary until we were safely landed in Sid Read's garden. There, Eric and I asked why we had been left out before. The older boys told us that they were frightened of getting us small ones involved again with Ikey Tooley and didn't know whether or not they could trust us to keep the secret of the place. It was Fairyland, and they didn't want it spoiled.

Eric and I fairly gasped. Young ruffians like Ray, Stanley and Sid talking about Fairyland! But we said nothing; we knew what they meant.

Time and again that summer we made our pilgrimage back to Fairyland, to the little lagoon and its beauty. I expect it has gone now, but I am deeply thankful that I saw it and was privileged for a season to fall under its spell.

Some readers may be reminded here of The Wind in the Willows and the place where Pan dwelt. It was not until a long time after that experience that I read that book, but I know exactly what Kenneth Grahame felt.

CHAPTER EIGHT

St Mary's Church

The Jesuit philosopher, scientist and theologian Teilhard de Chardin opines in his book *The Phenomenon of Man* that we are influenced in our formative years more by the 'passivities' of our lives, referred to in the preface, than by our 'activities'. By this, I take it that he means that we are more affected in our subconscious by happenings outside us but affecting us, over which we have no control and which we may not consciously appreciate, than choices of action which we ourselves initiate.

This is so true. With that thought I introduce the subject of our village church and the profound influence that it had, not only on my life but on those of my contemporaries. I am more than grateful to my parents, the clergy, the village elders and the people among whom I spent my earliest years for the atmosphere they created, which has guided my life ever since. The older I grow, the more convinced I am of the truth of this influence and its effects on my personality and character.

My contemporaries at Wroxham were wonderful people, all of them from highest to lowest, if I may put it that way. We children of the village were regarded by them as a trust. They cared for us and considered it a duty to correct us if it seemed to them that we needed guidance, and we never resented it, nor did our parents. Rather than saying to us "I'll tell your father and mother" they would say "Your parents would be very upset if they knew you were behaving like this". That is a far more telling and subtle way of instruction.

I did not know of this particular verse from the Bible when I was a boy, but it might well have been the guiding principle of my elders and betters:

'Thus saith the Lord, 'Stand ye in the ways and see, and ask for the
old paths, where is the good way, and walk therein, and ye shall find
rest for your souls:'
and the verse ends - and it is such a commentary on this permissive age:
'...but they said, 'We will not walk therein'.
You will find it in the book of Jeremiah, chapter 8 verse 16.

Wroxham Church, the Church of St Mary the Virgin (as was the legend heading the choir notices) was and is very dear to me, and I remember it with great gratitude and affection. I must have been very young, perhaps two or three, when I was first conscious of it. Mumma took me there with my sisters. My father and elder brothers were in the choir, and there I would sit in the family pew, sometimes on a hassock in the bowels of the pew, sometimes on the seat itself and sometimes on Mumma's knee, or cuddled by one of my sisters. Perhaps I would drop off to sleep in the sermon, but whatever was going on my inner self would be absorbing the ethos of my surroundings and the deep spirituality there engendered and enshrined. One always felt of Wroxham Church what Sir John Betjeman wrote of St Endellion's Church in Cornwall:

'Indeed the church gives the impression that it goes on praying
day and night, whether there are people in it or not.'

Such is the atmosphere of the Church of St Mary the Virgin, Wroxham.

The oldest part of the church is the Norman arch and doorway. It has stood since the monks of Caen built the original church. The rest of the building is nondescript, apart from its proportions, which like so many of the Norfolk churches are satisfactory and right. It must have been restored at some time or other very badly during the last two centuries.

Inside the main doorway to the left are the remains of a stone stairway going up through the thickness of the wall, which must have led at one time to a chamber over the porch where the visiting priest-monk would be able to find shelter. Possibly he came from the Cathedral monastery foundation in Norwich, or more likely from the great Benedictine Abbey of St Benet, way down on the marshes near Horning. He would have come up the river by a wherry of those days and landed just below the church, where one can see the river winding on its sluggish way through the marshes. The Bishop of Norwich still carries the title of Abbot of St Benet, and most Diocesans find time in the summer to make a pilgrimage down the river to the remains of the Abbey buildings.

Returning to the church; by the chancel arch in the left-hand corner of what is now a side chapel but which was in my early boyhood the choir vestry, there are the remains of yet another stone stairway, again leading through the wall to what must have been a rood loft over a screen, from which the Gospel would be read on high festivals. One can see on the south wall of the chancel where this stairway would have emerged. So there must be, under the modern plaster and brick or stonework, parts of a much older church over which restoration has smeared make-up, hiding the original building.

The church, like nearly all Norfolk churches, is built of flintstone, and stands near to the village of Lower Wroxham. It might be construed from this that the Black Death, which ravaged so much of East Anglia, must not have afflicted Wroxham very badly. Most churches in the neighbourhood are some considerable distance from present villages. This is because after the Black Death villages that clustered round the church and burial ground were burned down, and a new village built away from what they assumed was the source of infection.

But this is not a dissertation on the architecture and history of Wroxham Church, fascinating though such a study could be. Rather it is a record of its impressions on me and on my contemporaries. There are two interesting features in the graveyard, possibly unknown to most parishioners but discovered and well known to us choristers. We knew all about the churchyard and its gravestones. Every Thursday we had choir practice. The boys met at seven in the evening and the men joined us at seven thirty. We would arrive in good time, since Dadda, as choirmaster, was a stickler for punctuality.

In the summer we would fill up the minutes left before practice by wandering round the graveyard trying to decipher the inscriptions on the older gravestones. Flat against the east wall of the church is a slab recording the burial of a 'blackamoor', a native from the West Indies who had been a household servant, possibly a slave, in the house of a former Vicar, the Reverend Daniel Bedingfield Colyer, and had been baptised by him. On the north wall of the chancel there is a large crested white marble memorial tablet recording the life and death of the said gentleman. Times out of number when I have been sitting in the choir on the opposite side to this memorial I have filled in the long minutes of a boring sermon like David Copperfield by reading through the tablets on the opposite wall, and Mr Colyer's was one of them. I have heard since that he was a great benefactor to the village during his incumbency and that at one time he had some threepenny bits minted specially for some reason or another, known now by numismatologists as Wroxham Threepennies. They are now collector's pieces.

Not many outside our immediate group would know that there is another interesting gravestone on the edge of the pathway on the left-hand side, just beyond the main porch. We discovered this stone one choir-practice night in the summer, and were very thrilled with our find. It records the death of a man who was 'foully murdered'. This was exciting to start with, but as we cleared the moss and weathering of the stone away, we could make out that his murderer was 'quickly apprehended', tried and condemned to death and that he was the last criminal to be hanged publicly from the keep of Norwich Castle.

We scrubbed the stone and tried to decipher the whole of the inscription, plus the name of the victim and that of his murderer, but we were never able to manage it. Perhaps the present generation of choristers may succeed where we failed. The stone is still there, very much weathered. I inspected it a few months ago when I visited the church and the graves of my parents, and was still filled with the same curiosity to know the truth of it all.

As boys, if we needed any information on the history of the village, there were always one or two of the elders who would provide us with some kind of explanation. In the case of our murdered man, however, we seemed to come up against a blank wall of ignorance. Nothing was forthcoming. Nobody volunteered any information, even the venerable and bearded Harry, whose favourite saying when tackled on a point of village lore would be: "'That wasn't in my father's time, nor yit in his father's time, nor the one afore that", and then there would be a ponderous pause, a deep breath, and "but I remember....", and so a saga would be pronounced, with all the taggings of veracity in tone of voice and introduction.

No, not even Harry could help here; but there was one great friend of ours, one 'Fafa' Holman, a bent ancient of the village, still able to do a day's stint in the fields and always ready to pass the time of day with the juveniles. He loved children and delighted in our company, and was never too busy for a chat with any one of us. I remember when we were at a loose end and happened upon him that we would press him to tell us a story. Fafa would always demur at this with a bashful smile on his bewhiskered visage, but we knew that a little pressure would open up the floodgates of his memory and he would produce the necessary story – in fact, two stories, because he always gave us an encore.

Had the late Cecil Sharp, or any of his folklore contemporaries, been aware of Fafa's extraordinary stories, they would have been more than intrigued, because they were not told in any recognisable dialect or language. To us they were completely incomprehensible - they were almost gibberish - and yet that dear old man must have had some inkling of their meaning, for he recited them solemnly and with due emphasis and great relish, as though they did indeed proclaim some mighty truths worthy of declaration.

It is a great pity that tape recorders hadn't been perfected in those days, because Fafa's orations would have provided fresh studies for philologists and others of their ilk. The old chap must have learned to tell his stories in his quaint and lilting dialect by heart. Thinking back on them now, I feel they must have been told in some lingering remnant of a tongue spoken by the denizens of the hamlets hidden somewhere on the lonely marshes between us and Great Yarmouth. It was, indeed, rumoured that a race of people quite unlike our stolid Norfolk stock with our flaxen Norse colouring still dwelt in the heart of the marshes. They were said to be swarthy folk, avoiding contact with the native East Anglians, possibly Celts who refused to move in early days. They had their own language and customs and kept themselves to themselves in the remote and almost inaccessible fastnesses of their steadings in the saltings - the hinterlands of Great Yarmouth.

But that isn't the story I was about to tell. You will be waiting to hear the story of that man who had been 'foully done to death'. Who was that man, and how did it all happen?

As I remarked above, we asked Fafa, and after due deliberation and a deal of persuasion he told us what his father had once told him. The murdered man had been a young wherryman, and his assailant was another. Both were paying court to a fair damsel, the daughter of the publican who ran the inn, which used to be at the junction of the Marlpit Dyke with the main river at Marl Staithe. No trace is left now of the inn and cottages that once were there, yet I can clearly remember seeing the buildings there as a boy, and they were inhabited too. The Marl Staithe Inn was about two miles upstream from Lower Wroxham, and wherries which had loaded marl for the roads from the marl-pits nearby would tie up for a while, perhaps awaiting a berth or the right wind and tide.

One of these two young men, so Fafa told us, was of a fierce and morose appearance and with a sullen temperament that could flame quickly into ungovernable bouts of rage. He was madly jealous of his rival, his opposite in appearance and temperament and well liked by all who knew him. I never learned their names, but to make the telling of the story easier I'll call the angry one Sam and the happy one Joe.

Jealous Sam had let it be known up and down the river that the girl was his and no-one else would have her. He had heard of the favours offered her by Joe and had told all and sundry that if he met up with his rival he would 'deal with him'. Fortunately the movements of their respective crafts up and down the river carrying cargoes between Aylsham and Great Yarmouth usually kept them apart. Each man called from time to time at Marl Staithe, and each pressed his suit with the girl and her parents when time and tide permitted.

At last the inevitable happened; an encounter. Sam's wherry was bound upstream and Joe's was sailing down. It was winter, and a howling North Easterly was shrieking across the marshlands, lashing the poplars with flurries of snow and sleet and making movement on the river almost impossible and certainly hazardous. The skippers of the two converging wherries decided that the conditions on the river were too dangerous, and as Lady Luck would have it, the two vessels tied up alongside each other at the Public Staithe at Lower Wroxham, one facing upstream, the other down.

From the staithe, the rough roadway known locally as Sot's Hole led up to the village of Lower Wroxham, with its few cottages and the old thatched inn, the Wroxham Castle Inn, at the junction of the trackway from the Staithe with the main road to Norwich. At the time there were thriving malthouses by the Public Staith, together with cottages for the maltsters and their families.

The two skippers decided to stay aboard their craft, so that they would be ready and clear-headed for an early start on the morrow. The two younger men, Sam and Joe, separately climbed the hill from the staith to the inn. In the public bar the two young men met the locals and separate groups formed around them. They chatted and played cards and drank their beer, glowering at one another through the tobacco fumes. Neither man spoke to the other until the end of the evening, when Sam, who had been drinking rather more heavily than Joe, made a move to go.

As he was leaving he left he lurched over to Joe, shook his fist in his face and said, "You leave my girl alone, or it'll be the worse for you". Joe, unperturbed, replied, "Don't be so bloody stupid". As Sam went out of the door he shouted after him, "And may the best man win!" Sam paused in the doorway and muttered "You look out, I haven't finished with you yet". Joe answered with a full-bellied laugh and there, as far as those in the pub were concerned, the incident ended. However, they all knew of Sam's temper and advised Joe to take care not to upset him, and not to follow him too soon down to the staith.

An hour or so later Joe left, good-humoured, well fortified with the Castle's good ale and laughing at the warnings from the other occupants of the bar to look out.

Joe was never seen alive again. Sam, in a black rage, was waiting in the hedgerow at the top of Sot's Hole. With the elements in as wild a temper as Sam himself, all was set for a black and grisly deed. I remember this so well, since as Fafa told the story we were standing on the very spot at the top of Sot's Hole where the murder was said to have been committed.

Fafa told us that the body was discovered by some of the maltsters on their way to work the following morning. The threats uttered by Sam were remembered by the men who had heard them in the bar on the previous night and, as the gravestone records, 'the murderer was quickly apprehended'. Sam was tried and pleaded guilty, and as the stone said, he became the last man to be hanged publicly from the keep of Norwich Castle.

Fafa told us that the body was discovered by some of the maltsters on their way to work the following morning. The threats uttered by Sam were remembered by the men who had heard them in the bar on the previous night and, as the gravestone records, 'the murderer was quickly apprehended'. Sam was tried and pleaded guilty, and as the stone said, he became the last man to be hanged publicly from the keep of Norwich Castle.

The Castle was burned down when I was a very little boy, but Sot's Hole and the Public Staith are still there. Who knows the truth or otherwise of Fafa's story? Certainly we boys believed it, and none of us was very keen after that to be anywhere near Sot's Hole after dark on blustery winter nights. The unhappy ghost of Sam was to be heard bewailing his heinous crime, and woe betide any villager who saw or heard him – so we said, and so we believed.

I must go back to my early impressions of the parish church. From my perch on Mumma's knee, if we were early enough to church on Sunday mornings, I would mark Dadda in his cassock putting numbers in the hymn boards and I would see the choristers, men and boys, arriving to put on their robes. We had a very large choir for a village of our size, which only boasted 1000 inhabitants when I was a boy. Unless it was a holiday or there was extremely bad weather, there were usually 14 to 18 boys and eight or 12 men present in the choir. They would pack themselves into a curtained space at the east end of the south aisle and generate a sustained buzz of semi-subdued chattering. We would see the tatty red and black felt curtain that enclosed the vestry place bulging more and more as the latecomers pushed their way in.

Dadda would find the place in the lectern Bible for the lessons, which he more often than not had to read, taking turns with the churchwardens. From time to time, as the conversations in the vestry reached a peak, usually during a pause in the voluntaries from the organ, Dadda would hurry across to the curtain and push his face inside to shush everybody to silence. Sometimes even the vicar would break off from whatever he was doing and go across to appeal for silence, but when one thinks of the numbers enclosed in that tiny space, the noise was not surprising. When I was a very small boy the almost rhythmical bulging of the ancient curtain impressed itself upon my mind as being part of the necessary pre-service ritual, and I longed to become part of it.

At Easter, Christmas or Harvest Thanksgiving, when all choir members made a point of putting in an appearance, one was left in a state of wonder almost akin to that of watching a conjuror pulling ribbons out of a hat as the choristers emerged from their retreat. We marvelled as to where they had been able to stow themselves. It was a few years after these early recollections that the choir moved to more commodious quarters under the tower. These they had to share with the bell-ringers, which really didn't help things. Now the bell-ringers have their own floor just above the choristers in the vestry, so all should be peace.

I was allowed to join the choir when I was six years old. My two older brothers were already choristers. In 1911, the year before I joined them, the choir were practising for the Triennial Festival of Choirs, which was held in Norwich Cathedral. Ray and I were sharing the back bedroom of the schoolhouse at that time. The choir practised in the schoolroom, quite close to us. I would be sent to bed just after six, and at about half past six, the boys would arrive at the school for the first part of the practice – the school being used of course because it was warm and convenient – and the men would arrive about seven.

The main work for the Festival was an oratorio called The Song of Miriam, and although I have never sung it I think I could sing every treble note of it – not the words, because they were not distinguishable through the walls of the school, but certainly everything else. I never went to sleep until Ray joined me. I can remember the opening phrase and words of the oratorio, 'Sound the timbrels…' sung by the choir with great verve. I longed to be in the schoolroom practising with them, but was adjudged too young. However my importunity was such that I was allowed in on my sixth birthday, in March the following year, 1912.

Normally our choir practices were held in the church each Thursday evening. March 1912 was a cold and windy month in Norfolk, and it was still dark at seven. Like all choirs, Wroxham had its initiation ceremony for the neophytes, and even though I was the Master's baby son I had to go through the rigmarole. It was quite simple, but very unnerving. It consisted of the newcomer having to run three times round the church 'widdershins', that is anti-clockwise or against the sun. You had to do it alone, while the other boys clustered outside the churchyard gate. On the third circumambulation you had to pause at a grating set close to the ground on the north-west wall of the church and shout down it, not moving away until you heard 'the old ghost shout back'. Only when you had heard the voice of the ghost were you allowed to complete the run.

It was a scarifying business, and I was very frightened, particularly as there was no path down the north side of the church and we were told that this was the ghostly side, since suicides and unbaptised babies had always been buried on that side and these were the ghosts most likely to appear. The older boys told us not to be frightened, and said that if we saw anything we would only have to yell for help and they would come at once. I did my rounds, made my shout and was admitted to the choir.

I had better explain this grating, low in the church wall, down which we made our ghost call. It was actually a ventilation opening for the heating apparatus of the church, and if ever a crazy contraption was devised by skill of mortal man as an arrangement for warming a large building, this was it. The church was heated, theoretically, by a line of stoves set in the floor of the centre aisle. Below these stoves went a long flue pipe which eventually led to a chimney pipe going up the 80 feet of the tower at the west end, emerging as a squat chimney pot at the top.

There were, if I remember rightly, five of these stoves, which burned downwards. Yes, believe it or not, the verger had to light the fires upside down. A mixture of coke and coal would be put in first to rest on a grate over a flue; the sticks sat on the coal and coke and the paper and straw was at the top. You lit the fire from the top and it burned downwards, eventually, you hoped, igniting the coal and coke. The fumes and smoke, so the theory was, were drawn up the underground flue by the draught, ultimately to be discharged from the pot at the top. In the ringers' chamber at the base of the tower was a small stove which was lit first of all and which was supposed to create the initial updraught to get the other fires going. I can only remark here 'funny ha ha'. I have outlined the theory of the thing; quite naturally, when the paper and straw were ignited on all five stoves, a great deal of smoke would be bound to distribute itself inside the church. Even when the stoves were lit and going strong, which they did sometimes, fumes would flavour the atmosphere.

In addition to all this, if it should so happen that the wind was blowing strongly from the south-west across the river valley, the fires would go merrily, the bulk of the heat would go up the chimney with the strong draught and the fires, lit and stoked up on the Saturday evening, would be burned out by the time the verger arrived to prepare for the 8 am service. He would have to go through all the rigmarole of lighting them again before 11 am Matins, and the congregation would arrive to be greeted by a church full of smoke, a freezing temperature and a livid verger. If, on the other hand, the wind was in the east or north, there would always be a downdraught and the stoves would burn badly, filling the church with coke fumes. You could never win.

In the mornings in winter the church was always bitterly cold, but it never bothered us unduly. We psalmodied, we litanised, we sermonised and we blew on our fingers, and the congregation came and complained, but we always stuck it out. I can never remember the vicar saying "Owing to the cold and fumes this morning we had better abandon the service". It was always "O ye frost and snow, bless ye the Lord: praise Him and magnify Him for ever".

Later the stoves in the floor were removed and we had a hot water system installed. It was certainly warmer and more comfortable, but we did miss the coke fumes and the general confusion of the old system. All the excitement seemed to have gone out of life.

Those old stoves, inconvenient as they were, also constituted a general disturbance in the conduct of divine service. When I first joined the choir the verger was a patriarchal old gentleman called Mr Bush. He had a fringe beard, rosy apple complexion and a wonderfully kind manner, and we loved him. In the winter when the stoves were lit, the tolling bell for service would stop and the choir would emerge from their vestry and precede the vicar into the chancel. We would sing a hymn and the vicar would launch into Matins. With the giving out of the scripture sentence, old Bush would emerge from the ringing chamber under the tower with a bucket of coke. As the exhortation was read by the vicar, so Bush would attack the first of the five stoves, yank off the lid, stir up the contents, throw more coke on, crunch it down with his hobnail boots, always with a loose heel-iron, throw on the stove lid with a crash and proceed to the next one.

By this time we were kneeling and had embarked on the general confession, admitting to having 'erred and strayed like lost sheep', all to the accompaniment of the crashes, bangs, crunches and heel-iron tappings of Bush as he progressed up the centre aisle. He would usually conclude his stoking with a grand flourish on the stove in the chancel, and by the time we had got through the responses and the Venite he would have arrived back at the west end of the church again and all would be quiet for the psalms.

One felt that dear old Bush would be thoroughly satisfied in the knowledge that he had made inaudible, except to the individual worshipper, the whole of the penitential part of Matins. Dear Mr Bush! In the summers that followed his retirement at a great age he would sit on a stool on sunny days at the gate of his cottage just above the school, and we children would always give him a kiss as we passed by. It was a tradition and a salute to a great character.

I must tell one final story about dear old Bush. Dadda always said that it was one of the funniest things he had ever witnessed. It took place in the church one hot Sunday morning in July, just after the old box pews had been removed from the nave and chancel and before the choir stalls had been put into position. That puts the date about 1901. Bush as verger still had a position in the chancel on the south side by the vicar. Dadda, who at that time was forming his first choir, sat opposite.

Just above Bush's head was a tall leaded window with a long sloping sill at the bottom, the width of the chancel wall. On this particular morning, just as Morning Prayer started, a swarm of bees arrived and clustered outside the church at the top of the window arch above the spot where Bush was sitting. Service had started and nothing could be done about it. It ought not to have worried anybody, but unfortunately a small diamond-shaped pane of glass had been broken at the top of the window close by where the bees were swarming. Some of the bees crawled in through it and, stupid as bees are during a swarm, lost their hold on the slippery glass and tumbled down to the sloping sill, where they rolled and fell to the floor and began to crawl aimlessly about.

By this time the service had progressed as far as the Litany. The vicar, a Mr Boddington, was reading the service. Bush, in his duty as verger, was making the responses, kneeling close by him and becoming increasingly aware of the large number of bees crawling on the floor round him and the vicar. He must have decided that something must be done about it before he or the vicar got stung. He didn't wish to disturb the conduct of the service, so he waited until the moment when, in his gruff deep Norfolk voice, he was to lead the congregation in the response "We beseech Thee to hear us, good Lord" and then leaned over from his stool and with his huge horny thumb cracked as many bees as he could reach.

The result was decorum during the vicar's petitions, alternating with mayhem during Mr Bush's responses. Dadda, opposite, witnessed all this going on and was almost ill with suppressed laughter. The vicar, aware that something was afoot, suddenly saw what was happening, and his voice trembled dangerously as he made his petitions. The congregation, warned by the tone of the vicar's voice, also saw, and they too were convulsed. By the time the Litany had been completed, the only unperturbed person in the church was Mr Bush, upright in his place and surrounded by the corpses of more bees than one could count. Dadda told the story many times, and rocked with laughter every time.

Our standards as a choir at Wroxham were very high. Visitors to the church would remark on our abilities. Dadda was very proud of the fact that more often than not, at the Choral Festival in Norwich Cathedral, we were placed in the first three of the Diocesan choirs after the Cathedral choir.

I have remarked before on the training Dadda had received as a chorister in Sheffield. Prior to his coming to Norfolk he had taught for a while at the Royal Caledonian School in London, and while there had further broadened his musical knowledge by joining the evening Voluntary Choir of St Paul's Cathedral and had sung and been trained there under Sir John Stainer and Sir George Clement Martin. There he was enabled to observe methods of choir training and voice training and generally enlarge his knowledge of church music. This knowledge he used with great effect in forming his choir at Wroxham.

Mark you, he was in a most privileged position as headmaster of the village school. Getting boys for his choir and training them was almost 'laid on' for him.

We prided ourselves on the fact that we sang everything except the Communion Service. One of the regrets Dadda always had was that owing to the ecclesiastical climate of St Mary's, which was 'Low Church', a sung Communion was not approved of, but we managed to sing everything else. In my early days there was no curtailing of the psalms of the day to the present insipid diet of one short psalm per service: we sang the whole of the psalm of the day, morning and evening, with the changes of chants as proscribed in the old Black Cathedral Psalter. We sang the Canticles of course, and the responses, and our repertoire of hymns was very extensive.

On festival high days we would sing special settings of the canticles and put on an anthem. Our repertoire of anthems was not large, because copies of them cost money and this was not easily come by; the Churchwardens held the purse strings and were not very forthcoming with the necessary cash. Nevertheless the yearly Choral Festival book did give us at least one anthem and a setting of the Magnificat and the Nunc Dimittis per year.

As a very small chorister, six years old, I used to find the pointing of the psalms a difficult problem - but then so did the rest of the choir, particularly the adult members. I used to get terribly worried and upset to the point of tears when I couldn't grasp what was happening, couldn't find the place or didn't know the tune or the words being sung. I remember disgracing myself on one occasion and getting a very black look from Dadda in consequence. It was one Sunday evening and for some reason or other I cannot recollect the vicar, in his notices, to everybody's surprise, suddenly called for the Doxology to be sung in thanksgiving for some 'mercy vouchsafed'. a) I didn't know what the doxology was; b) I didn't know where to find it and c) nobody seemed to be prepared to come to my rescue.

I burst into tears. Dadda frowned at me, which made me even more tearful, then, being unable to find my handkerchief, I committed the apparently unforgivable sin of wiping my face with the sleeve of my surplice, to the intense amusement of the rest of the choirboys and the extreme annoyance of Dadda. I got a wigging after the service and my brothers and sisters, who were always irritated by my tearful tendencies, were very scathing over the whole episode.

The point I want to make here is the one I stressed at the beginning of this chapter; the regular recital of the psalter at morning and evening prayer, the regular following of the Lessons. We used of course the old 1871 lectionary, which took one through the Old Testament about twice a year and the New Testament more than three times. The lessons were long and complete. Where in these days can you expect to hear the complete story of Nebuchadnezzar and his brass band – sackbutt, psaltery, flute, dulcimer, harp and all kinds of music? We heard it regularly each year as the session went round and would follow it in our Bibles, the places found beforehand. This wonderful literature would be absorbed by us and appreciated. There are parts of the Bible which even now I can repeat off by heart: passages that I never deliberately set out to learn but which became part of me through the regular recitals, year by year. They were 'passivities', if you get my meaning.

Our vicar of the time about which I write was one William Hewetson, known familiarly to us as Billy, though not when Dadda or Mumma were within earshot. We were never allowed to speak familiarly of the Parish Priest or to criticise him. Billy was an old-fashioned Prayer Book Evangelical, if you understand the meaning of that. We marked the church's year sedulously and carefully. He would never miss a Saint's Day or Holy Day and one would see him pedalling down Church Lane on his push-bike, later on his motor bike and finally in a fearful-looking and fearful-sounding three-wheeled buggy which was guaranteed to shake the living daylights out of anybody inside a mile.

Rain or shine, Billy would be at church. He had two parishes to serve, and right well he served them. In church we always had the Athanasian Creed on its proper days, and we sang it. I doubt whether many of today's young incumbents have ever said it, or indeed know of its existence.

In Lent Billy would always lay on week-night mission services, illustrated by lantern slides. These services were eagerly looked forward to by the congregation and were very well attended. We choirboys liked them because of the novelty, and because we sat down in the nave. On the screen were thrown the words of great Moody and Sankey favourites, the like of which did not appear in the sober selection of Hymns Ancient and Modern. We loved to roar out 'Tell me the old, old story'.

Talking of this, I remember once having an organist in my service days in Orkney towards the end of the Second World War who flatly refused to soil his fingers and the organ by playing that hymn. If I wanted it I had to play it myself – and mark you it was to be played from that highbrow of highbrow hymnals, The English Hymnal. I confess I gave way to him. The service was just about to start when he issued this edict, and it rankled.

Dadda used to manipulate a magic lantern, illuminated by a fearful device which generated acetylene gas. There was some story to the effect that Billy Hewetson, the vicar, on one occasion, Dadda being indisposed, had to work the apparatus himself. He forgot the instructions he had been given and the safety precautions enjoined upon him and the whole thing blew up in church; but that was well before my time. I can only recall the fact that he flatly refused to have anything more to do with it and always gave it a very wide berth when it was in action. But we did enjoy our Lantern Services.

Wroxham Church had two quite different congregations, for the morning and evening services. Each was composed of different, yet equally good churchgoers who backed things up wonderfully.

In my early days there were, in a good number of the bigger houses, large staffs of domestic servants. It was not always taken into account that Sundays were also a day of rest for the servants. Their masters and mistresses would attend Divine Service in the morning while lunch was being prepared, and then the domestics would be permitted – no, expected – to attend church at night, but we were always sure of a good turnout at either service.

At one time the butler at the Hall, who was an Anglican, would walk the three miles or so down to the village to attend Evensong. We dearly loved our evening service and in the First World War when the lights had to be darkened, the evening congregation, aided by old sails and bits of tarpaulin from the boatyards, blacked out the main windows of the church rather than forgo it. It was family worship, particularly in the evenings. We were eight in family. The Chamberlains at the Post office, before three of their boys were killed in the war, were 12 in number. The Stevensons turned out nine on parade, and so I could go on. Outside the church after service the village would gather and natter.

We had a Sunday School, which used to meet in the village school about half an hour before Morning Service. We had that half-hour of instruction in the faith, 'a text for the week' had to be learned by the little ones and the collect for the day by the older children. When Sunday School was over we would crocodile down Church Lane for Morning Service. Apart from those who broke out of the crocodile to join their parents in their pews or go into the choir vestry, we all sat at the lower end of the north aisle. Those not in the choir or with their parents would leave in the hymn before the sermon.

As far as the Sunday School choristers were concerned, Dadda thought that attendance at Sunday School, plus choir and full Morning and Evening Prayer might tend towards spiritual saturation, even spiritual indigestion, so we were excused Sunday School.

Two excellent spinster ladies, the Misses Preston, ran the Sunday School, and they did so in a most orderly and proper fashion. They visited parents and took a keen and benevolent interest in all our doings. I can remember one amusing incident concerning Sunday School, although it didn't seem funny at the time. The vicar was away on holiday and his locum was an enormous Cockney parson from some parish in the East End of London. He had a great black beard and the loudest voice I think I have ever heard in any parson. To hear him sing All Things Bright and Beautiful, as he did with us on this particular Sunday morning, was to hear the whole of the Handel Choir of the Alexandra Palace in London in their fullest spate. He was terrific.

He boomed into Sunday School that morning and asked if he could have a word with us, which he did, spreading himself in true Cockney fashion. In the course of his remarks he stated that there were only two verses in the Bible which mentioned the words 'boys and girls' and challenged us to find them. We were wildly excited, and we all milled home after church to get at our Bibles. There must have been more Bible reading done in the village of Wroxham during that week than ever before – or since – but nobody could come up with the answer, and we were all in despair.

Then came the breakthrough. Mrs Chamberlain at the Post Office suggested to her children that they should look in a Concordance that she had found in an old bookcase. A quick reference to this excellent book produced the answer, but her children were much too generous to keep it to themselves, so one or two close friends were told, under the seal of the strictest secrecy. They of course passed it on to their friends, and so on. As a result of which, by the following Sunday every member of the Sunday School, which was a large one and which on this day produced a bumper attendance, had a little piece of paper scribed with the books, chapters and verses required.

Believe it or not that wretched parson never turned up. He had returned to London, and we saw no more of him. We never trusted a Cockney again.

What are the scripture references for those verses? You must look them up for yourselves. Try a Concordance as the Chamberlains did.

This chapter has been a mixture. Starting with morality, it has meandered through a galaxy of remembered incidents and scenes. As I started the chapter, so I would like to end it. Again my theme concerns Sunday School, or rather a by-product of it, the monthly children's service held in the afternoon. This was never a great success, as neither the vicar nor his curate had any idea of how to deal with children. Fortunately for them, we were naturally a well-behaved lot. However on one occasion Billy Hewetson produced one of those 'passivities' which in later life has often come to the surface of my subconscious and enlightened my understanding. In the church in those days, behind the altar table at the east end of the chancel, there was some rather fine carved oak panelling. The ravages of woodworm, age and other pests have destroyed it and I gather it had to be burned, but in my young days there it stood. Framed within the openings of it were some panels painted green with gilded lettering on them declaring the Ten Commandments, the Apostles' Creed and the Lord's Prayer. At one of our children's services Billy Hewetson suddenly asked, a propos of nothing at all, why these particular passages should be so prominently displayed in the church. Well, we all guessed various things: that one could read them when one had little else to do; one could learn them off by heart: or you could read them at the appropriate place in the service without having to follow in the Prayer Book, and so on and so forth.

Billy let us all have our say. Then he stopped us and said very quietly: "Something of what each of you have said is true, but I'll tell you the real reason why they are there. They are reminders that if you forget God's Law (he pointed to the Ten Commandments) "and forget your Faith" (he pointed to the Creed and then to the Lord's Prayer) "and your prayers, what happens is what you see in the centre." He pointed to the cross on the altar.

"There is crucifixion, not this time of Jesus in Palestine, but crucifixion of the whole human race."

He was so right.

CHAPTER NINE

Singing and ringing

Some words from a well known modern carol, *Ding Dong Merrily On High*, set the scene for this particular chapter. They go:

'Pray you dutifully prime
Your matin chime, ye ringers:
May you beautifully rime,
Your eve-time song, ye singers.'

I have remarked ad nauseam what singers we were at Wroxham, and I cannot leave this part of my remembrance (and this is really an extension of the previous chapter) without recounting a story to underline it.

In the spring of 1942 I was returning to England from Bermuda, where I had left the RN cruiser in which I had been serving. The merchant ship in which I was sailing was the Shaw Saville boat Mataroa. She was making a homeward voyage from Australia and had called at Cape Town and Buenos Aires. Her cold storage holds were full of much-needed meat carcasses for starving Great Britain. She also had on board large numbers of women and children returning to the UK from the early fever of evacuation which had scuttled them overseas at the beginning of the war, and which hadn't pleased them.

We were doing about 12 knots, zig-zagging, of course, which delayed our progress. Because our cargo of meat was so essential we had been routed by the nearest way, which was outside the convoy shipping lanes. We were therefore unescorted, and steamed on our lonely way hoping not to sight anything at all.

Naturally all we adults were very nervous, and our state of mind was not improved by the knowledge which had leaked through to us that a German battleship was reported to be 'loose' in the North Atlantic, and the seaway was thick with wolf packs of U-boats. You may remember the surge of U-boat activity at that period of the war. We wondered what we would do with all the women and children should a torpedo hit us. It was not a nice thought.

We menfolk volunteered to man lookout posts by day and night with binoculars, in a search for the telltale plume of a U-boat periscope. Mataroa would have been a rich prize for any U-boat skipper and we were sure our departure would not have gone unreported.

My watch was from 2 am to 4 am in the middle watch and my lookout post was on the boat deck, starboard side. There I would stand in the warm darkness, my eyes glued to the glasses, looking for the wake of a periscope or the track of a torpedo. The unaccustomed need for wakefulness in the dead hours of the night and the soporific effect of the movement of the ship through the phosphorescent water made keeping wide awake something of a problem. I solved it by engaging in a mental exercise which gave me great pleasure and kept me awake and alert, and here is where the first part of my title for this chapter comes in. I sang through all the settings, anthems, carols, chants, hymn tunes and oratorios I could remember from my boyhood chorister days. *Smart in F, Stanford in B flat, Praise the Lord, O Jerusalem, The Lord is my strength and my shield, Angels, ever bright and fair* – lots and lots of them. Each night as I stood there on watch, I would try to recall one more of the songs of praise I had learned in my youth.

I can remember singing to myself a carol we particularly loved when we were children. The copies we had in the choir were very tattered and torn and there were only enough of them to supply the men. We boys had to write out the words on paper and keep them as our copies. I don't know either the author of the words or the composer of the tune, but I have a feeling it must have been brought from Sheffield by Dadda. I never remember hearing it sung anywhere other than Wroxham. The words are typically

Victorian sentiment, the melody haunting and sweet. I will include what I can remember of the words here. Perhaps somebody may read this and know the carol.

> *Sweeter than songs of summer,*
> *The time of blossom and bird;*
> *The beautiful midnight music*
> *In the flowerless winter heard:*
> *Sweeter than songs from far lands,*
> *But gladder than all, they bring*
> *The song of the Christmas angels*
> *With news of a holy spring.*
>
> *They tell of a little tired one*
> *Laid on a Maiden's breast,*
> *Who says to the heavy laden,*
> *'Come, I will give you rest'.*
> *See I am meek and lowly*
> *Hasten to learn of me*
> *And deep in the midst of labour*
> *The peace of your souls shall be.*

That's the first time I have written those words down since preparing for a Christmas carol service long ago.

But I must finish my story of the voyage of the *Mataroa*. We had left Bermuda for home on a Monday, and when the following Sunday came along, with the ship in mid-Atlantic, the Captain sent for me. His name was Lucky Jackson; he had sailed ships in both world wars and never lost one, which was a comforting thought. Captain Jackson asked if I would take Divine Service in the lounge on Sunday morning. He would have to be on the bridge, otherwise, as is the custom of the Merchant Navy, he would have taken it himself. I was honoured to be asked and took the service. Everybody, including the seamen off watch, was there. Everybody had felt the tension of our position and the need for help. As the Americans used to say on Okinawa "You don't find atheists in fox-holes", and we were very much in a fox-hole.

I told the folk on board of my watch-keeping ploy, my singing and how close it seemed to bring me to a certainty of God and His care. I meant that from the bottom of my heart. Do you know, they all said that all care seemed to be lifted from our shoulders. I had finished my short talk to them with the last words of that lovely carol that I had remembered up there on the boat deck:

See I am meek and lowly
Hasten to learn of me
And deep in the midst of labour
The peace of your souls shall be.

Throughout the whole of that fraught voyage we saw no threat to our safety from any kind of enemy action. We sailed up the Clyde almost as if we were a day trip returning from the Isle of Arran.

This passion for singing which occupied so much of our activity in Wroxham was all inspired by the enthusiasm and expertise of Dadda. My paternal grandfather, a native of Shropshire from whence on marriage he had emigrated to Sheffield, had a passion for music beyond the norm. Dadda used to say that the old chap had begotten children without any thought other than an ambition to have a family string orchestra. Any of his children who lacked a flair for strings was out, as far as Grandfather was concerned. Dadda was one of those misfits, but he had developed his talent for voice training and choir training, and well he used it.

Towards the end of his life Grandfather moved to Norfolk, and occasionally he would come and stay with us. He always brought his cello with him and my eldest sister, Marjorie, would have to play the piano parts

111

of Beethoven cello works for the old boy. The whole household would be hushed to silence while this operation was in progress; not a door must slam, not a floorboard creak, not a voice be upraised which might interrupt the music being conjured in the drawing room. Poor Marjorie would get the cello bow across her knuckles if she made a mistake, and Mumma would go nearly crazy with frustration.

Dadda used to tell a good story against Grandfather. Apparently when they were living in Sheffield he would organise a small orchestra of family and friends and offer to conduct and back up the organ in local churches, whose choirs, as is the custom in the north, would put on a performance of Handel's *Messiah* at Christmas or Easter, or *Elijah* on other occasions. One Saturday before a Sunday performance, grandfather's cellist was taken ill and rushed into hospital. This was a disaster of the first magnitude, since Grandfather could hardly play the cello and conduct as well. Then somebody volunteered the information that the cellist who had just joined the orchestra at the local music hall was familiar with the *Messiah* (who in Sheffield isn't?) and would be willing to play. Grandfather went round to see him at once. The cellist was delighted to help out.

All went well. The cellist was all that he claimed to be and Grandfather was delighted. Then a snag – just before the chorus, *Lift up your heads O ye gates*, a string snapped. The cellist hastened to repair it as the rest of the orchestra and the choir plunged into the chorus. When they reached the great climax, *Who is the King of Glory?*, the orchestra sawed valiantly away, the choir lifted up their voices, and the cellist, still struggling with his string, was heard muttering under his breath to the huge delight of all in his neighbourhood, "Who's't King o' Glory? Wairt till a get this string fixed. Ah'll show 'em 'oo's 't King o' Glory".

According to my Aunt Jane, if Grandfather wanted a 'set o' band parts' and one of the children needed a new pair of shoes, and there was only the money to satisfy one request, the band parts always won. He was a formidable old gentleman whose last gesture to the claims of music was (though he could ill afford it) to have a whole hymn tune - soprano, alto, tenor, bass – carved on the stone over his wife's grave, together with the four verses of the hymn. You can see it there in Salhouse churchyard, the neighbouring village to Wroxham, marking his last resting place. You can see where all the music came from.

Although, in those days, pay for an amateur choir such as the one at Wroxham was virtually unknown, we did not go without our perks. There were two great occasions in the year to which we all looked forward with great anticipation. One was the annual Choir Outing to Great Yarmouth in the summer and the other was the Choir Supper at Christmas. The slender coffers of the church provided the necessary funding.

The excursion to Great Yarmouth was a tremendous event. In the early days we would catch a train from Wroxham station, change at Whitlingham (no station there now), or at Norwich Thorpe and arrive in a state of great excitement at Vauxhall Station, Great Yarmouth. There we would be briefed by Dadda as to the place and time for lunch – always at the same hotel – and warned not to get lost. We younger fry were told to keep with the older boys, which, of course, didn't please our seniors. But such was our sense of loyalty that we never got lost or lost anybody.

Our first excursion was always a trip down the harbour to Gorleston and back. In those days there was a small fleet of double-ended steam ferry boats, which ran a non-stop service from a place near Haven Bridge to Gorleston near the mouth of the harbour. The fare was quite cheap, about sixpence. We would pile on to one of those boats and be thrilled by the sight of the fishing fleet, a Norwegian timber ship or perhaps a Royal Naval fishery protection cruiser in the harbour. The tang of the salt water, the malty smell of a big brewery there, are with me now. The sight of the ships and the busyness of the harbour always thrilled me. I wouldn't have missed that trip from my itinerary for anything and I'm quite certain that it was from these occasions that I ultimately got my desire to exercise my ministry amongst 'they who go down to the sea in ships'.

In the afternoon there was always a visit to the circus at the Hippodrome, usually organised by Mr Bird, one of the tenors in the choir and a great favourite with all of us. It gives me a thrill even now occasionally to see on TV that circus in the Hippodrome at Yarmouth, still going strong each summer but now lacking one turn which always ended the performance, the thrill of seeing the circular arena sink and water bubble through to make a swimming pool in which there would be a water ballet as a grand finale.

From the Hippodrome to the Pleasure Beach with a daring ride on the Scenic Railway, still in being, and so to tea and the train and home, all of us playing the mouth organs or toy trumpets we had bought. It was a wonderful day always and we never seemed to strike bad weather.

One never-to-be-forgotten day it was decided that we should go to Great Yarmouth down the river. Messrs Alfred Collins' boatyard had just launched a new motor day-cruiser, a splendid boat called *Broadland Belle*. It is still in commission, but this was to be its maiden trip. We all piled on board at 8 am; we needed the early start since Yarmouth is 27 miles downriver and, at an average speed of about six knots, it would take quite a time. Unfortunately the engine didn't seem to be up to its job, and we had a lot of trouble with it both going and coming. Mr Jack Powles, who has since given his name to one of the largest boatyards at Wroxham, was there, as an apprentice engineer. He would have remembered the occasion. In spite of the setbacks we all thoroughly enjoyed the trip. We sang all the way there and all the way back, arriving in Wroxham somewhere near midnight, all dead tired but very happy.

The Choir Supper, usually held in the schoolroom just after Christmas, was our other great event. It gave the village an opportunity to show their appreciation of our labours in the choir; and how they rose to the occasion. The great and the lowly housewives of the village combined to reward us with the best banquet their kitchens could provide. The trestle tables, borrowed from the Castle Inn, quite literally groaned under the weight of the good things provided. Mumma was the organiser of the feast. The tables were laid and decorated by other ladies from the village. It was a wonderful 'blowout' to which everybody who had anything at all to do with the running of the church was invited; bellringers, sidesmen, verger, everyone was there.

After we had sung grace came the meal, and I couldn't begin to describe the 'feast of fat things upon the lees' that was provided. There were crackers and nuts and fruit and everything that would make for a festive occasion.

After the supper, when we had cleared all the tables away, Dadda, as Master of Ceremonies, would organise our entertainment with round games in which everybody joined, and with individual items contributed by the various talented members of our community. There were time-honoured games like 'The Family Coach' and 'Stirring the Pudding' and so on. A barrel of beer was provided in the Infants' Room for the men, out of sight of us innocents. We all had a wonderful time.

The highlight of the evening's junketings always came just before the end, when Dadda and Mr Phil Steventon, our leading tenor, would join forces to sing together Balfe's famous duet *Excelsior* with all the glutinous sentiment that could be dragged out of it. Yet how we loved it, and how we cheered them to the echo, together with the providers of the feast, before the vicar's blessing to speed us on our way. We loved our singing, and all that went with it – and I haven't told you the half.

And then there was the ringing. It was a great day in my young life when curiosity, prompted by the keenness of my ears, led me to enquire about the sound of our church bells and how it was produced. I would have been about 10 at the time. I had noticed that sometimes before morning or evening service, instead of the six bells of the church just tumbling around, one-two-three-four-five-six, there would be a preface to the actual ringing when, in a cacophony of sound, each bell would appear to vie with its fellows in a glorious nonsense of noise. Then there would be a silence, and suddenly the brazen monsters would start to ring in grand and logical chorus, first into straight rounds and then into complicated changes which had no specific recognisable tune, but to the listening and discerning ear, would seem to progress in a methodical order.

For some months I listened to this. None of my contemporaries in the choir seemed to know much about it, or even bothered with it, and the bell-ringers themselves were a remote body of grown-ups. I was much too shy to ask what it was all about. Even Dadda, who was usually my compendium of all knowledge, failed to enlighten me.

There seemed to be only one way of finding out, and that was to hang about the belfry before the ringing started and pick up what information I could by on-the-spot observation. This stratagem was aided by the fact that winter was approaching and on Tuesday evenings, one would hear the bells again as the ringers practised, peeling in full chorus and sometimes for a long time.

So, one Sunday morning, I got down to church early. The bells used to start to ring about half an hour before the time of service, and I watched what happened. Gradually the bell-ringers sauntered up to church. I never saw one of them hurry, they were always slow moving and very deliberate. I believe I once saw one of them arrive on a bicycle, but even that was a ponderous business. Anyway, the men arrived, passed the time of day, looked at watches and, when six of them had assembled, they went into the church and behind the curtain which hid the ringing chamber from the rest of the congregation. There the bell-ropes hung with their multi-coloured 'sallies', handgrips woven into the ropes, to hand.

One of the men would say "Well we might as well get 'em up", and so saying he would grasp the rope by the sally and start to pull heavily. The bell to which the rope was attached would start to speak way above in the belfry, first singly and then appearing to answer itself. And so with each of the bells in turn, each ringer handling his own bell-rope. I was fascinated, and when this preliminary flourish sank to silence, I said to one of the ringers who had noticed my presence, "Do you think I could try that?" He laughed and said, "Come down on Tuesday night to our practice and see whether you can manage a bell". They then started to peel the bells in rounds and swung into changes as the conductor bade them. Occasionally he would call the mystic word 'Bob', or sometimes 'Single', and the sallies would dance up and down in the ringing chamber as the bells gaily rang out above.

I couldn't wait until Tuesday evening. Ray said that he would come with me, and having got Dadda's permission, off we went to the church. Here the ringers were assembled and we were briefed. First we were told never to touch a bell-rope until we had learned to ring and had, so to speak, passed our apprenticeship, since bell-ropes handled by the ignorant can be killers. We were then told to arrive early on practice nights, say half an hour before practice commenced, and one of the ringers would be there to teach us how to handle a bell. As an earnest of their consenting to teach us, we were each allowed, under the instruction of one of them, to 'pull a bell off', that is, the bell having been raised to its ringing position, to pull on the sally, take the five or six hundredweight bell above you in the tower off its balance and feel the whole thing come alive in your hands. It is a terrifying yet exhilarating experience when felt for the first time.

As the weeks passed by we practised carefully. We were taken up the tower into the bell chamber to see how the mechanism worked so that we would know as we controlled our bell-ropes what was happening 60 feet above. It took the whole winter to become proficient in handling a bell, and it was a proud day when we first joined the band of ringers on a Sunday morning to peal the bells for Matins. Sam Nunn, the venerable captain of the tower, said that we had done well, but there was still much to learn.

Throughout that summer we turned up at practices – there were not many in the growing season, for there were gardens and allotments to be tended – and we rang or chimed on Sundays depending on how many ringers turned up. Some of them acted as skippers on the yachts let by the boatyards, and naturally they couldn't be in two places at once. Taking it by and large, one could depend on Sam Nunn, Charlie Kidd, Harry Spurgeon, Ray and me to be there, so we usually managed to chime the six, even if we hadn't enough to ring.

Then the following winter we started to learn 'method'. Change ringing on a peal of bells is one of the most wonderful exercises in concentration that one could ever experience. It took us a long while to realise that the ringing of changes was not something that one did by ear or memory of a 'tune', but something that had to be controlled by the eye. The standard work on change ringing is a book by Jasper Snowdon called *Rope-sight*. Sam Nunn gave me his treasured well-worn copy, and I have it still. The multi-coloured sallies that one grasped in ringing, which danced up and down as the peal progressed, were not just convenient handgrips but visible signals to tell all taking part what the bells above were doing. You followed the up and down movements of the sallies, not the noise the bells were making. In the exercise of this observation lay the secret of method change ringing and it took a very, very long time to learn.

During that winter, besides being at practice on Tuesday evenings, we would go down to the malt-houses by the Grange, where Sam Nunn was Foreman Maltster. Here we would sit round the glowing fire under the kiln, eating handfuls of malted barley and, with pieces of stick, we would learn the elementary principles of method and rope-sight; up to simulate hand stroke, down to simulate back stroke. It was fascinating, and we talked and thought bell ringing till the family must have been heartily sick of it. But we undertook faithfully to go early on Tuesday evenings in all weathers to light the oil lantern in the ringing chamber, to kindle a fire in the little bogey stove in the corner and to keep the ringing chamber clean and tidy. We counted ourselves privileged to be allowed to do it.

I suppose mastering the intricacies of change ringing technique and method took us all of 18 months, but then one can never say that one has learned all. The one thing campanology does is to give the devotee a fever to get your hands on the bell-ropes of as many rings as you can. It never leaves you. To this end, with our fellow ringers, we started our travels to the various towers in our immediate district - and Norfolk is lavish with its towers and its bells. We usually travelled by bicycle, or, if funds permitted, in Phil Steventon's coal lorry, hooded, swept and garnished and with two forms inside to sit on.

One of our first visits was to Coltishall, the nearest tower to us and one possessing six bells, though heavier than ours at Wroxham. I can remember on drowsy evenings hearing the Coltishall bells at practice. The sound would drift across the river valley some four or five miles as the crow flies, ponderous, heavy and slow. They would mingle with the piping of the peewits across the marches, and I can never hear the piping of peewits to this day without hearing again Coltishall bells. We found them heavy to ring when we visited the tower and met the local ringers, but we rang our '700' (the number of changes that can be rung on six bell is 720), and were tolerably satisfied with our performance.

For some reason or other the next tower we visited was at Stratton Strawless, with its six bells, but what I particularly remember about the place was that we were asked not to ring between 5.30 pm and 6, and just before 5.30 would we please toll the tenor bell for five minutes. We did as we were requested. Sam Nunn tolled the tenor and we walked out of the church and its yard towards the village.

On the way out we passed the Rector going into church, an elderly dignified figure in cassock and cape. The bell ceased and Sam came out and joined us. I was curious about what went on in church and so, making some excuse or other, I went back in. There was somebody speaking, and I realised that it was the Rector saying Evening Prayer to himself, or so it seemed to me. I had never experienced this before, and when I reached home I mentioned it to Dadda. He immediately produced a prayer book and pointed out the directions to all beneficed clergy contained in the preface, which reads:

And the Curate that ministereth in every Parish Church or Chapel, being at home, and not being otherwise reasonably hindered, shall say the same (i.e. Morning and Evening Prayer) in the Parish Church or Chapel where he ministereth, and shall cause a Bell to be tolled thereunto a convenient time before he begin, that people may come hear God's Word and to pray with him.

Thank you Stratton Strawless for that revelation, and I would that every 'curate' had the same discipline and perseverance in prayer as that old Rector.

Round about this time Happisburgh ('Haseboro') parish church on the coast had its bells restored and rehung, and we went over to be present at their hallowing by the Bishop. We joined in the celebrations and rang a few 'touches' to get the feel of the bells and to record our visit. I remember being much impressed by this gaunt church, with its high tower overlooking the North Sea. At a place called Haseboro Gap there are some of the most treacherous sandbanks and currents. As the bells sounded over land and sea, I wandered round the churchyard looking at the tombstones and remarked on the numbers of graves of 'unknown seamen' whose bodies had been washed up on the shore after some storm to be reverently buried in this windswept churchyard. I mused on how those bells ringing their joyful peal overhead might be heard by passing ships, or perchance be solemnly tolled as some 'unknown seaman' was borne to his last resting place. Morbid thought? No, not really, only the very active imagination of a young romantic adolescent stirred by the music of the bells.

The great 'Wool' church of Tunstead is not far from Wroxham, and there they have a peal of eight. I doubt very much that they are still rung today, for the tower housing them was in a very shaky state when we visited them just after the 1914-1918 war. The vicar of Tunstead at that time was himself a ringer and he was delighted to welcome us. He eventually joined us in ringing, taking a rope and thoroughly enjoying himself. When we set the bells up at the end of the 'touch' he started to walk away from his ringing position, and found that he couldn't move. Immediately behind him, unnoticed by any of us, there was a large and ominous crack in the masonry of the tower, which, apparently, opened and shut as the tower swayed with the ringing of the eight bells. This crack had captured a fold of his cassock, and he couldn't get away. We had a really good laugh over this incident. We had to ring the bells again to open up the crack and let him go free. I think it was then that the good folk of Tunstead woke up to the fact that something needed doing if their tower was still to stand.

But what a church! It was like a young cathedral, set in miles and miles of farmland with hardly a house to be seen. It is served now by a vicar who lives some distance away and has four other churches to care for. It must now be a very long time since those lovely bells sounded in a peel over the flat lands of Norfolk.

Several of the boys joined us in ringing; Stanley and Eric Stevenson, 'Apples' Coffin and Sid Read learned to 'man the ropes'. That is why I am so certain that the 'passivities' thus absorbed in my early years have had such a profound influence upon me. Singing and ringing - what a marvellous insight my contemporaries and I had in the practice of the externals of our worship. I am more than grateful to Wroxham and its folk for all that they gave me.

And as for the bells, as the Psalmist says, 'They have neither speech nor language; but their voices are heard among them'.

CHAPTER TEN

Down the Avenue

When we were children, Caesar's word informed us that Gaul was divided into three parts. So was Wroxham, as we saw it in my early years. First there was the village itself, known as Lower Wroxham. It was self-contained and had its pub, school and church. I have already written largely of it, and although it is bound to intrude from time to time in these memoirs we will leave it at that for the moment.

Secondly there was 'Down the bridge'. This part of the village was geographically in the parish of Hoveton St John and hence not strictly Wroxham, although it contained Wroxham's railway station, the Post Office and the famous Broadland stores known as Roys of Wroxham. In my young days this was a comfortable business consisting of the Groceries, the Ironmongery and the Drapery in their several orders. The steam flour mill by the bridge was Wroxham Flour Mills Ltd and all this area, belonging largely to the boating interests, was known as Wroxham.

From time to time the patriotic inhabitants of the Hoveton part of the village would almost raise a cry of 'no surrender' to the Wroxhamites and vaunt the claims of Hoveton St John, but little would come of it. It would have been difficult to change, given that all the public services had for years been labelled Wroxham.

When I was a boy, the place where the largest building of the Roy complex of shops now stands was a piece of waste ground. Twice a year it would be visited by a strange and primitive travelling show known as Rhubub's Fair. This featured a hand-turned barrel organ, minus monkey, a half-dozen or so ratty swingboats, one or two stalls containing cheap and tawdry fair trinkets and garish china ornaments, and a sweet stall where one might see rock being made. I believe sometimes there was a fish-and-chip stall, and it had the inevitable shooting gallery and coconut shy. The proprietor, Rhubub himself – heaven alone knows what his actual name was – was a gypsy, brash, huge in girth and a real character. His family, who manned the stalls and ran the show, were typical of their kind.

As children we were forbidden to go anywhere near the fair. Hearing the jangle and trills of the barrel organ we would long to slip down the road to see the 'bright lights' (naphtha flares of course) and taste the forbidden fruit, but we never did. We were too well known, and our appearance there would certainly have been reported to Mumma, who, I should imagine, had ideas that some of her brood might be abducted by the dreadful gypsies. Goodness only knows how they could have got away with anybody, since their transport was dependent on a few weary horses and a couple of mangy donkeys, and they never travelled more than a few miles from North Walsham. Also, of course, Mumma was convinced that the whole set-up was a travelling flea circus.

'Down the bridge' was a mile from us, and apart from using its railway station or patronising its shops occasionally (Mumma mostly shopped in Norwich) we rarely played in or visited that part of the village. Yet I do remember one fleeting visit to Rhubub's Fair. Ray and I had been to Norwich with our parents, and we begged to be allowed, as we passed the site on our way home, to walk round it. Dadda and Mumma, to our surprise and delight, consented, and we were allowed half an hour while they called on some friends. We were given a few pence and permitted to look round, with strict injunctions from Mumma not to go near any of the caravans.

Off we went in great excitement. Ray won a coconut, so we were able to return to our parents after half an hour or so with some profit to show for the expenditure of our pence. It was very comic when we got home. Mumma was so convinced of the verminous state of the fair that we had to have a bath with carbolic soap to wash away any infection we might have taken.

Talking of fairs, we would be taken each Easter to the huge Tombland Fair held from time immemorial outside the Cathedral gates at Norwich. This fair was indeed something to visit, garnished as it was with all the latest fairground novelties and machinery. I can remember standing entranced in front of the great 'fair-organ' of Messrs Thurstons' huge roundabout and marvelling at its stentorian voice. It combined with half a score of other fair-organs on other roundabouts, so that the whole air was filled with the raucous sound of the reedy voices of myriads of pipes.

I could stand and watch for hours the powerful fair-engines, those magnificent steam locomotives in their bright livery and highly-polished twisted brassware, working silently with hardly a hiss of steam, driving the dynamo in front of the funnel to provide the electric current for the bright lights of the roundabout. We would buy and devour brown and white ginger fair biscuits and come home tired out and almost intoxicated by the marvels we had witnessed. In the playground at school we would play 'fairs' for weeks afterwards.

As I write of these treats, I am reminded of a most curious incident. I can't give it a date, but I think I must have been about six or seven years old at the time. Bostock and Wombwell's Menagerie was coming to Norwich and Ray and I and the two Stevenson boys had been promised by our respective parents that if we were good, we would be taken to see the animals.

I was wildly excited at the prospect of seeing live elephants, lions, tigers, monkeys, giraffes and all the rest of the fabulous animals I had read about in geography books and seen pictured in various illustrations. This excitement on the Friday immediately before the Saturday treat had its effect on my behaviour in school, and this eventually so irritated my teacher, at that time a girl from Salhouse called Gertie Wright, that she made me stand on the form with my hands on my head.

This was dreadful. I had already been in trouble with Dadda at home at lunchtime and I knew that if he paid a visit to our class and saw me standing on the form, my bad behaviour would lose me my treat to Bostock and Wombwell. I was in a state of near panic. What was I to do?

Now I know this story sounds improbable, but I can assure you it actually happened. Gertie Wright, that morning in our scripture lesson, had been talking about saying one's prayers and how one should not be afraid to ask God for anything, no matter how trivial, because He always understood and would help those in trouble, even though they had been the cause of the trouble themselves. She had backed up her statements by quoting various relevant texts in Holy Writ. I remember being most impressed. All this came back to me standing on my form expecting disaster. I remember thinking to myself, "there's no harm in trying. He can only say no". So I closed my eyes very meekly, and with my hands together on top of my head, I asked God in my childish way to let me get down off that wretched form if I'd promise to be good. I said something like "Please God, may I get down from this form and I'll be a good boy. Amen."

As I opened my eyes, bang on cue, Gertie said, "You can get down now Clifford, and get on with your work." I gasped and gulped, and a very frightened little boy clambered down off his seat and resumed his work. A few minutes later Dadda walked into the room. I had been saved in the nick of time. I've never told that story before to anyone, but I can assure you that it was quite true and that it was, to say the least of it, unnerving.

But I've bumbled on about all kinds of things. I have not yet got down yet to the actual subject of this chapter, this third division of our village, 'Down the avenue'.

If you went out of the front gate of the schoolhouse and turned left down Church Lane as if you were going to church, but, when you reached the corner, instead of bearing to the left, you turned sharp right and went over the railway bridge, you would see in front of you The Avenue. This road is indeed an avenue, of magnificent beeches. Some of them alas have gone, old age and weather having taken their toll, but some still stand as grand and venerable sentinels on both sides of the road. The bark on most of them has been scored by generations of carved initials and love tokens. The Avenue has always been the chosen courting ground of the village.

In the days of my boyhood, The Avenue was the real 'West End' of

Wroxham. The 'money' lived down there, in palatial houses and large riverside bungalows. As you walked down the tree-lined path, a road to the left would take you to two of the boatyards, those of Ernest and Alfred Collins, brothers, but not partners. There were one or two big houses down there. Miss Agnes King had the entrance to her house there, and so did the Hansells. Mr Peter Hansell, son of that house, was tutor to the then Prince of Wales, later to become Edward VIII, and when Mr Peter was visiting his father and came to church, we choirboys would regard him with great awe and reverence and almost feel like bursting into the National Anthem on sighting him. Funny kids we were.

Also down the first turning and on the corner of a footpath which led back to the main road stood a magnificent Beech Tree (I have put that in capitals because it deserved it). The beech is gone now, but what a tree it was.

However, returning to The Avenue proper, a few hundred yards walk from the first turning brought one to the second turning and down this road, which ultimately led one to the shores of Wroxham Broad, lived the real 'nobs'.

When I first took note of the 'Who's Who' of Wroxham, our local MP, a staunch Liberal called Sir Frank Price, lived in one of the first houses on the left. Next to him was a most respectable Scotsman, a Mr McMinn, and his wife. Mr McMinn was a churchwarden and a manager of Dadda's school. He wore a long and very dignified grey beard and always dressed in impeccable Victorian style. He would visit the school to check the registers, always accompanied by Mrs McMinn. This redoubtable lady, the soul of kindness, always carried round with her a large grey parrot in a cage. It had a knowing eye. It could be coaxed by her to speak, but more often than not it would maintain a sulky silence. Possibly this was because it would get no rewarding titbits from us.

I remember once encountering Mr McMinn when I was playing with Eric in the lane just below the school. I guessed he was going to see Dadda, whom I knew to be out. Politely I approached the old gentleman and said: "Please sir, are you going to see my Dadda?"

He said he was, and I told him that Father was out. The old gentleman thanked me most politely and went back down the lane smiling, broadly. It came back to me afterwards via Dadda that the old gentleman had thought me a very polite and helpful little boy. My brothers and sisters, however, regarded my intervention as a bit of cheek.

A little further down the same side of the road lived the Clarke family. Mr Clarke had built a lovely riverside house with fine gardens and lawns and inlets from the river for his boats. He prided himself particularly on his black-enamelled 'half-decker' boat, which he cared for as a child and in which he sailed in the various regattas on the river. He would catch the same train into Norwich that we schoolboys caught for schools in the town. He always walked the two miles to the station from his house and it used to be my delight on a frosty morning, to walk behind him down to the main road, savouring the aroma of the excellent after-breakfast cigar he would always smoke.

Beyond the Clarke's was the house of a Mr Passmore, again in a lovely riverside setting of gardens and greensward. Mr Bird, one of the tenors in the choir, was gardener here, and, when the Passmores were away it was a great treat to be invited down there to tea with Mr and Mrs Bird, both of whom adored children. After leaving the Passmores' the road dwindled to a narrow track and passed over a number of very shaky bridges before reaching the last bungalow, on the edge of the Broad.

Now, returning to the Avenue, just past the second turning, but this time on the right, two stately iron gates opened into a drive which led down through fir plantations and a glimpse on the right of a wide park, to Wroxham House. Wroxham House and its sweeping parkland, with some of the most magnificent sweet chestnut trees I have ever seen, with its copses and thick planted woods of conifers, have all departed into the hands of the developers, and what I tell now is of something irrevocably gone, something that exerted a wonderful influence on the boys of our village. It was a most gracious house, occupied by a wonderful couple whose goodness to the village I don't think was ever fully appreciated, except by us boys, who knew we were very fortunate to have had such people to show care and affection for us.

Colonel and Mrs Charles were not natives of the village; they had moved into Wroxham House early in the century. The Colonel was an old friend of Lord Baden Powell, with whom he had campaigned in South Africa. Mrs Charles was a Scot by birth and lineage. I was always told that the considerable fir plantations that surrounded the property had been placed there by the good Colonel in order that Mrs Charles, who loved her Scotland, should have a reminder in our flat Norfolk of the trees of her native land. 'Apples' Coffin (why we ever called him Apples I can't think), who was gardener's boy at Wroxham House, used to poke great fun, behind his back I'm afraid, at the Colonel, who liked nothing better than to go into his woods with a 'slasher' and trim the lower boughs off the trees. 'Snedding' they call it in Scotland. Apples used to complain that the old Colonel made more mess than was helpful and that he always had to clear this up.

The head gardener and his wife were also Scots, and were as hospitable as their master and mistress. It was a most heart-warming place, and we all were very lucky to have the run of it.

The Colonel, as I have said before, was completely sold on the Scout movement founded by his old friend Baden Powell. He became the first County Commissioner for Norfolk, and his infectious enthusiasm for scouting spread to all the boys of the village. The Colonel provided us with a terrain for the practice of our scoutcraft. We had the run of the whole of his considerable acreage, which on one side extended right along the borders of Wroxham Broad, part of which he owned.

He also provided us with a wonderful headquarters known as 'The Den'. This lay fairly close to the Avenue but was screened from it by a thick plantation of young conifers. The Den was a shed which at one time had been the estate carpenter's shop. It had two rooms, the first of which, with a hard packed floor, was our meeting place. Here we gathered on one or two nights each week to conduct our indoor scouting business. There was a large open fireplace in one of the walls and on cold winter evenings we used to gather wood from the copses around, as we were permitted to do, and make a fire that would have roasted an ox.

Dadda was Scoutmaster, and the under gardener at Wroxham House, a Mr Lane, was Assistant Scoutmaster. We did enjoy our scouting. In those days it hadn't been spoiled by the town-bred interferences of the London Headquarters. In our way we were very efficient. The Colonel saw to it that a scout evening would never pass without his looking in in a most friendly and quiet way to see how we were getting on. He knew all of us by our Christian names, and we always behaved to him with the respect he deserved.

The other room of the Den contained the old carpenter's bench, where we sometimes assayed to make things. I once made four rough forms, I remember, for seats for the Den. The Colonel had provided us with a kit of tools which we could, and did, use. This second room of the Den had a thick coat of fine dust on the floor. Goodness knows where it came from. Time and again we tried to get rid of it, but we never succeeded. There was a fair-sized field close by the Den where the Colonel erected goal posts so that we could play football. Our football matches against other teams were however few and far between, since there were no other organisations like ours in any of the neighbouring villages.

The Colonel was an old Harrovian and a devotee of cricket. Solemn matches would be arranged on the field in the summertime. They were never a great success because, in spite of his enthusiasm, we none of us really cottoned on to the game. I think the Colonel must have been quite disappointed, because he took a lot of trouble over it, even creating nets where he would coach us.

In the old stables and harness rooms of the house was stored all our camping gear, which was pretty extensive, and we also maintained in one of the better rooms a large wardrobe of articles of scout uniform. To this day I can never smell mothballs without being reminded of that 'quartermaster's store'.

Most of our gear, bell tents, cooking equipment, large steel 'trek cart' and all the rest of the camping impedimenta had been purchased from the proceeds of Scout Concerts arranged by Dadda. These were always good and were packed out by the appreciative villagers. Dadda's standards of amateur entertainment were high. He always reckoned that if a member of the public paid a shilling for a ticket, a lot of money in those far-off days, he deserved a shilling's worth of good entertainment for his money, no different in effort from that he would expect to find on the stage of the Norwich Hippodrome. So there would be no hiding behind amateur status to excuse mediocrity and real hard work and expertise had to be put into the show. We never went on to the stage unrehearsed or not knowing our lines.

Gang shows had not been heard of in those days, but in our small way I have no doubt at all that our shows were every bit as good as those put on in later years by the famous Ralph Reader. Certainly the village thought so, and I am not indulging here in vain boasting. This sort of attainment was part of the uniqueness of our village.

We always had an annual Scout camp, except for two summers during the Great War when we couldn't get permission from the authorities to erect our tents. Our favourite camping spots were Bacton and Mundesley on the Norfolk coast. Both destinations involved the transport of all our equipment from Wroxham House to the station in our trek cart, loading it on to the train as far as North Walsham and unloading it again to get it over to the old Midland and Great Northern Line station, mercifully close by, loading it again on to the train for Mundesley, or (for Bacton) to Paston and Knapton, a station set in the midst of a howling wilderness of flat fields of corn. One wondered why the station was ever put there, but that was our alighting place if Bacton was our objective.

The trek from Paston and Knapton to Bacton was about four miles of hard going with our trek cart, loaded as it was with tentage and baggage, and each boy had a fairly large pack for his own personal belongings and blankets. We had never heard of sleeping-bags; blankets and pins were our remedy for keeping out the draught. If we were making for Bacton, we would have to stop for an al fresco meal at midday.

At Bacton we would camp on land belonging to a most hospitable farmer, a Mr Cubitt, who was always more than helpful. Around the farm lay the scattered ruins of Bromholm Priory, and we always found a deal of interest in exploring and clambering over them. Bacton then had a stretch of most marvellous golden sands and when the tide was out, wonderful pools in which to bathe. We fed well and slept well, except of course on the first night, when nobody sleeps. We played the most fascinating games on the beach and in the surrounding countryside, some of them night games, which were always great fun. Mark you, we always kept a wary eye on the Priory ruins in case some marauding ghost-monk chose to make a manifestation.

On the day we were to be inspected by the Colonel, we always had a sand-modelling competition on the sands. He would reward us with useful prizes, usually consisting of some item of scout equipment, and, for the best-kept tent a smashing cake made by the cook at Wroxham House. They were fabulous times. We always preferred Bacton to Mundesley, although the latter was easier to get to. Bacton was a village and Mundesley a small town, and we preferred the simplicity of the village. Besides, the camping site on Mr Cubitt's farm was ideal. The greater part of the expenses of the annual summer camp would be met from funds raised by Dadda, so that the boys themselves had little to contribute in the way of hard cash.

In addition to these annual camps we had weekend camps in the woods around Wroxham House. These were always carefully watched by the Colonel, who would drop by from time to time to satisfy himself that all was well and ship-shape and that we were comfortable. In spite of his declared policy that we should fend for ourselves larder-wise, Mrs Charles would usually arrange for some delicacy or other to be sent down from the kitchen at the house.

There was another side to the Colonel's character, and his care for us should not go unrecorded. Besides his great interest in our physical and mental welfare, he considered it essential that our characters should be trained and guided. To this end, in autumn, winter and spring, we would gather on Sunday afternoons in his study in Wroxham House. There, in front of a blazing log fire, we would sit or lie on the floor while our Colonel would read to us and discuss a chapter or so of his famous friend's book *Scouting for Boys* (rarely read by scouts today, even if they have heard of it). We thoroughly enjoyed these sessions and it would have to be really bad weather or perhaps a bad cold that would cause any of us to miss the 'Scout's Own', as the Colonel called it.

Like so many of the 'passivities', they made a lasting impression on us all. Mrs Charles would come in at the end of the hour and we would choose a hymn, which she would play on the piano. Usually, if he was there, a verse would be sung by Rodney Press, one of Dadda's choristers, who had a phenomenally beautiful voice. The Colonel would say Grace, Mrs Charles would distribute 'sweeties' all round and we would depart for home. A very treasured memory that, and a tribute to a great man.

While on this subject of our spiritual welfare, if I may put it that way, I must mention our church parades. These were always presided over by the Colonel and Mr Lane, the assistant Scoutmaster, and were held monthly, mostly in the winter. Dadda was always fully occupied in the church getting ready for the morning service, so he took no part in them.

We had two side drums, a big drum and half a dozen or so bugles. In order not to appear too military in our parade we always marched in single file, each patrol headed by its Leader and Second. The buglers and drums only really got off the ground during the latter days of the war, when a sympathetic regular Army bugler, billeted in the village, took us over and trained us. Most of us were much better drummers than buglers, but this good man sorted us out.

We would start out from the front gates of Wroxham House after having been inspected by the Colonel and march up the Avenue towards the church. The one or two Methodist boys would peel off towards the Methodist Chapel when we got to the main road. The rest of us would continue on towards the church, arriving there with a great flourish. Then those of us who were in the choir would rush into the vestry and throw on our cassocks and surplices, unable on these occasions to wear our celluloid Eton collars. We would process to our places in the choir stalls feeling strangely undressed, with our khaki shirt collars showing above our black cassocks.

After church we would fall in outside the churchyard. Admired by the various members of the congregation there assembled, we would then march off in great style back down the Avenue to be dismissed by Mr Lane, and perhaps be rewarded with a sweet or a piece of shortbread by Mrs Charles to round off the morning. Our church parade was never looked upon as a disagreeable chore. It was part and parcel of our bringing up. We trusted that our elders and betters knew what was good for us and did it without complaining.

I cannot leave the Avenue without one more memory. A former occupant of Wroxham House had constructed a roadway from the house, across the road and into the woodlands, leading down to a small staithe and a boathouse on the fringe of Wroxham Broad. This roadway was known as the Private Avenue, and no mere words of mine can describe its grandeur and peace. The road went straight down towards a gateway leading on to the marshes through an avenue of trees of all kinds and colours. There were birds of all kinds, squirrels, rabbits and other wild creatures all enjoying this haven of peace. The roadway itself was covered with a soft carpet of bright green moss. At all times of the year, standing at the top end of this track, one's breath would be taken away at the sheer beauty there in evidence. The impression made on me by the vista of this quiet walk was most profound and lasting. I could never enter on it without stopping to gaze on the scene and to savour the full glory of it.

A final memory of the Avenue which I feel I must include. It is on a very personal note that I must give a grateful thought to another household, humble and yet very dear, and as valued to me as any other remembrance. Harry Lane, a tenor in the choir, Assistant Scoutmaster and a gardener at Wroxham House, lived with his wife and two daughters in a pretty cottage on the estate not far from the big house.

Mr Lane and his wife kept a wonderful open house and their hospitality in their way was as lavish as that of any other person, high or low, in the village. As a boy I spent numbers of truly happy evenings in that humble home, together with a number of my contemporaries. We were always welcome, playing most hilarious games of 'Find the Lady' and laughing uproariously. Mrs Lane was a wonderful cook, whose triumphs in the culinary art came from an 'oven in the wall'. In case you don't know how that works in the modern age, let me tell you that you lit a fire in the oven with a faggot of dry wood and shut the oven door on it, leaving it to roar itself away to ashes. Having prepared all your dishes needing cooking, you would then open the door, rake out the red-hot embers, and into that inferno of heat you would place your bread, cakes, biscuits, buns or what-have-you. You would leave them for the correct time and then remove them. If you have never sampled that sort of cooking, then neither Savoy, Ritz nor any other cuisine can ever capture it for you. All you need is a cottage, a wall oven, a faggot and a Mrs Lane, and there you'll have it. But, as the poet says, 'A rainbow and a cuckoo, Lord' don't come together very often.

Mrs Lane would bring the evening to a close with hot mugs of milky cocoa, a plateful of her heavenly cooking and a generosity to us all. The party would be made up by Apples Coffin, Alfie Harmer, who had been badly crippled in the Great War, but was always a keen scout, Peggy and Connie, the two girls of the household, Mr and Mrs Lane and me, plus one or two others. We so enjoyed the wonderful freedom of those evenings that I cannot let this record of 'Down the Avenue' close without tribute to them. They, like so many others in that unique village, were wonderful and lovely people.

CHAPTER ELEVEN

To be a farmer's boy

So far in these recollections of my boyhood I have talked much of our singing, of church, of our social life and home. But we did have other concerns.

I was eight years old when the Great War burst on Europe. When this sudden change in our lives and fortunes got home to me, I asked for an explanation. We were at the breakfast table. It must have been early on in the war, round about the time of the retreat from Mons. Dadda was reading the morning paper and gloomily reviewing the situation to my elder brother and sisters. I felt out of things and wanted to be enlightened and so, catching sight of a headline in the morning paper, I asked, "What's it all about Dadda? Has Mr Asquith declared war on the Prime Minister?" You can imagine the ribald laughter from my brother and sisters. They almost went into hysterics, but Dadda, also laughing, explained as much as he thought I could take of how things were.

This led to thoughts of war work. Mumma, who had for years been a keen worker in the British Red Cross movement, immediately found her métier. Dividing her time equally between her school work, her household, her nursing and what rest she could get, she was more than fully occupied.

This was even more so when a convalescent home for soldiers was opened 'down the bridge'. It was called St Gregory's and did yeoman work, in which Mumma was fully engaged in her 'spare time'. How she managed to fit in all that she did still mystifies me. She had endless energy.

She bought a tricycle, to our great amusement, until we realised what a boon it was to her in the to-and-fro journeys between home and the hospital, which was over a mile away. Often, when there had been an influx of patients, it would be the early hours of the morning before she got home. She had been in a bicycle accident some years before and had lost her nerve on that machine, hence the tricycle was just right for her – and for us too. It was kept in the school lobby and when Mumma was out we had a great time with it riding round and round the schoolroom.

Eric Stevenson and I were having a wonderful game one day. We were a train, I was the driver and Eric, standing on the back axle, was the guard. In the middle of all this Mumma arrived home unexpectedly and, hearing our noise, walked into school and caught us red-handed. My word, we got a wigging. I had it worse, because Eric was the younger and therefore I must have been the instigator. Funnily enough it was only a month or so ago that Eric reminded me of that incident and the 'tongue pie' we got. I'm afraid it didn't stop us. We still, when opportunity offered, had our fun with it. I used to love being asked to ride it down to the station to meet Mumma off a train.

However, this is not getting any more forward with my subject. As I remarked above, Mumma did her bit for the war effort, the girls sewed and knitted and my eldest sister, like her mother, was connected with the Red Cross. Stanley, my elder brother, was caught up with the senior scouts and night patrols. We weren't far from the coast, so there was always a scare of spies and invasion. Dadda was also in the Red Cross and the Volunteers. Ray and I seemed to be the only ones left out and we felt we ought to be allowed to 'do our bit'.

I don't quite know how it happened, but Mr Stephen Sutton, a local big farmer who at that time rented Hill Farm and its rickyard (I have mentioned this farm before in connection with Farmer Howlett and the Caen Meadow), called in one morning at school and had a long conversation in the boys' lobby with Dadda. The upshot of this was that Ray was called out of his class and went out into the lobby with Dadda and Mr Sutton, and a few minutes came back in blushing and looking very pleased with himself. I was in the class below him, so I wasn't near enough to be able to ask him what it was all about – and I was dying to know.

After morning school was over and we went in to dinner, Dadda announced to us all that Ray was going to do some war work. Mr Sutton the farmer had called at school to ask for help at Hill Farm. The 'call-up' had taken his labourer for that farm, and could Dadda recommend a reliable boy. Dadda, remembering our requests to 'do something', had recommended Ray. He was to go that evening after school to the farm, where Mr Sutton would explain to him his duties. Naturally, I begged to be allowed to go with him and so, when school was over, we both trotted up to the farm. Remember Ray was 10 and I was eight.

We found Mr Sutton waiting for us. He was one of the biggest farmers in our district, with property in about four villages. He was an 'old-type' farmer in that he always rode a horse around his farms. The horse was there, tethered to a gatepost, and Mr Sutton was busily engaged in feeding some young calves with a mixture of roots, chaff and flights (husks and barley beards). As he continued with this, giving each of us skeps to carry, he told Ray his duties. I know this will take some believing, but I can assure you of its truth.

First, there were 26 head of young stock, bullocks and heifers. These lived in a large barn enclosure in deep litter and had to be fed twice a day with roots, chaff and flights mixed together. The hayrack had also to be kept filled with hay. I forget how many skeps were carried for them, but it seemed as though it worked out to about one per head of stock. The roots had to be cut in an antique hand-turned chopping machine and the chaff cut in an equally ancient piece of old Ming. The flights were kept loose in another shed and as much as was needed was fetched and carried.

The flights were brutes. They would get into one's clothes and work their way through to the skin, where they would irritate abominably. Then, when Mr Sutton gave the order, Ray was to muck out the calves' enclosure, putting the manure on the midden close by. Then he had to carry fresh straw from a straw-stack in the rickyard some distance from the barn. He also had to pump a supply of fresh water into troughs for their drinking.

There were also six cows in milk to be tended. These, in the summer, grazed on the two pastures close to the farm. Every now and again, when Mr Sutton thought the time was ripe, Ray would have to take them down the Church Lane and turn them into the Caen Meadow to give the other two leys a rest. These cows had to be fetched in and let out again each morning and evening, when six calves were brought to them for suckling. The enclosure for the calves had to be kept clean and well littered, and so did the stalls for the cows. Hay had to be put into the racks in the stalls for the cows to feed on when suckling the calves and buckets of drinking water provided. In the winter the cows were allowed out only during the day and were kept in at night, which meant, of course, that food and drink would have to be provided in case they wanted a snack during the night, which of course they always did. And they always made a considerable mess in their stalls, which meant more 'mucking out' in the morning. There wasn't a dull moment.

Mr Sutton's original idea was that Ray should do all this himself. Granted, if he had nothing else to do all day, he might have managed it inside 24 hours, but, since he had to go to school it would mean that from about 6 am until about 10 pm he wouldn't be able to stop except for meals and school. Ray had sufficient sense to see this, and, keen as he was, he pointed this out to Mr Sutton. The farmer saw the point at once, thought a moment and then turned to me.

"Is this your brother?" he said to Ray, who replied that I was.

"Will he help?" I spoke for myself and said that I would.

"Right then" said Mr Sutton. "That's settled. You can both start tomorrow morning. I reckon you'd better get here about six for the morning feeds and come up after school for the evening ones and the mucking-out. I'll come in and see how you're getting on about once a week and I'll see that you get all the roots and hay you want. Be careful not to let the stock out on to the roads, or they'll take you a dance half way across the county."

That last warning proved only too true. On the very few occasions when a door or a gate was left open, the young stock was out before you could say 'knife', and it was the devil's own job to get them in again. Talk about the Gadarene swine.

The farmer departed, after showing us where to find everything and how to get hold of him if we needed help. He told us to collect our wages from his house on the main road at the same time as the labourers collected theirs. That was on a Friday afternoon after work. Have you any idea what those wages were? I'll wager you haven't. Our pay was one shilling a week for Ray and sixpence a week for me. We considered ourselves millionaires. But we did all that work and carried all that responsibility for two years.

It was the hardest manual labour I have ever done in my life. To be up there at the farm by 6 am, dark and bitterly cold in winter, and having to do everything by the light of a hurricane lamp was an experience I will never forget. It took us several weeks to work out a satisfactory and labour-saving routine and we were both, I remember, very fair in our apportioning out the work.

The cutting of the roots and the chaff, a back-breaking job with the primaeval machines we had at our disposal, we did in the evenings. We could take our time over it. We would get up to the farm straight after school and set to work on our evening feeds with the necessary turning of the handles of the cutters. In turn, evening by evening, one would do the chopping while the other looked after the cows and calves and did the fetching and carrying.

Before we set to work on the stock feeding, we would fetch the milch cows from the meadows and put the calves to them. Sometimes, particularly in the winter, the cows would be clustered round the farm gate lowing and yearning to get into the protection of the byre, the food, the cosy straw and the cover. But in the summer they could be devils incarnate. No amount of "Come , come, come, come, come" would coax them away from the lush green grass. They had to be fetched and driven, the brutes, and then, if they weren't watched, they would take it out on the young calves in revenge for having been brought in. The idea was that we would feed the young stock while the cows and calves got on with their business. At least, that was the theory. One could never trust them. The devils had to be watched the whole time, so, the routine worked something like this:

First we would put the hay in the racks for the cows and fill a bucket of water for each of them. Then one of us would start chopping while the other fetched in the cows. As soon as the cows were in their stalls and tethered and the calves out to them, the one on 'carrying' duties would set to work to fill the mangers for the young stock, every now and again stopping to look at the cows and calves to see that there had been no difference of opinion over the suckling. That would be the morning and evening routine. In the evening, after the cows had been put out to pasture again and the suckling calves returned to their enclosure, we would set to work to do all the chopping for the following morning feeds and would fill all the racks with hay.

Often we would have to go back again after tea to finish the work. The great thing was to make the morning work as light as we could. Usually we kept the cow and calf places as clean as possible during the week, leaving the mucking out of the young stock, an Augean Stables job, for Saturday mornings. Thank goodness we had little or no interference from Mr Sutton the farmer. He always seemed satisfied with all that we did – and so he should have been, at 18 pence a week.

Looking on the brighter side, it was great fun having the whole of the farm buildings as our private domain. When we first explored the complex of buildings we found what might almost have been described as a secret room behind the old stables. It must have been a room where the horse-keeper of the old days kept his posh harness, his horse medicines and his spare clothes. The door was quite difficult to locate unless you knew where to look. It was set in the panel boarding surrounding the inner stables and we only found it by accident. There was a good old-fashioned fireplace in there and some old worm-eaten chairs, and we made that room our retreat. We would always light a fire in there on winter evenings and occasionally roast some potatoes. With some favoured friends, Eric of course and Stanley, his brother, and one or two others, we formed a 'Secret Society', and this became its headquarters.

There were one or two cornfields in the immediate neighbourhood of

Hill Farm which during our two-year stint were planted with cereals. In August they would be cut, harvested and stacked. The corn stacks were built in the old rickyard of the farm. Chasing the rabbits at harvest time and being given a share to take home, rationing being what it was, was very popular with Mumma, although none of us relished the job of gutting and skinning them. Dadda usually had to complete that chore.

A great time of activity at the farm was the arrival of the threshing tackle, which always seemed to happen in late autumn or early winter. A steam traction engine, threshing drum and straw elevator would arrive in the afternoon to be set up ready for threshing to start first thing in the morning. The foreman always had to take care that the threshing drum was level – it wouldn't work otherwise. The engine had to be put at exactly the right distance so that the driving belt would be neither too slack nor too tight. The straw elevator would be manhandled into position so that the straw stack would rise just where the farmer wanted it. When the foreman was satisfied, the fire in the engine would be damped down for the night, the thatch on the stack would be removed and all would be left in readiness for the morning, everybody praying that it wouldn't turn to rain during the night.

Before daylight the following morning the men would arrive, half and half threshing crew and farm labourers. Each man would be detailed to a particular job. Wagons, tumbrils and their attendant shire horses would arrive to cart away the sacks of grain, and there would be a spare horse to fetch water from the river in a clumsy-looking tank on three wheels to supply the thirsty engine with drink. The engine man would have stirred up his fire and got a good head of steam and when all was ready, a signal would be given, the engine would start and the drum would commence its ear-penetrating, throbbing hum, which could be heard all over the village. The straw elevator would start its 'clank-clank-clank' as the forks which conveyed the straw on to the stack jerked up their trackway, and we would be off.

Ray and I used to have the job of recovering the flights which shook out under the drum, filling an empty tumbril supplied for that purpose, and then leading the horse round to the shed in our part of the farm buildings, where they would be added to the store of food for 'our' stock. Everybody would stop every now and again to chase the great rats as they were shaken out of the sheaves or the diminishing stack. There wasn't a dull or a lazy moment on threshing day.

The threshing operation always seemed to fall on a day when there was a biting east wind which nearly cut your head off as you came round from the sheltered side of the drum, stack or engine and met the full blast of it. So much did this weather hazard impress itself upon me that I remember writing some verses about it during the Second World War years, which went something like this:

There's wind-frost in the countryside
In the threshing time of year,
When the fingers lose their feeling
And the bird has lost its fear:
When winter leaves blow willy-nill
And hedgers hug the fire.
There's wind-frost in the countryside
And sweet straw in the byre.

After two years hard labour at Hill Farm, we reluctantly had to give up our jobs. As I have remarked, Ray left Dadda's school and went to Norwich as a day boy. I couldn't carry on single-handed, and nobody would take Ray's job on. Mr Sutton the farmer was very upset about it, since the whole organisation had to close down and Hill Farm no longer ran stock.

We both missed the work and our contact with the animals, particularly the cows - faithful and patient beasts at most times, though at others they could be most infuriating. Yet each cow had a personality, and we gave them all names. One particularly curiously-coloured beast (it was a mixture of blue, white and bluey-grey), with some sort of Jersey ancestry, we called Polly. She was our favourite. This silly, affectionate beast would do her best, as she walked up the lane from the Caen Meadow, to insinuate her head under the arm of whichever of us was in charge of herding that day, so that Ray or I would come at the end of the slow plodding procession with an arm round Polly's neck. This would cause tremendous amusement in the schoolhouse as we passed and we would be chaffed about it afterwards when we got home.

I was quite sure that one of our charges, a 'polled' cow, deep brown in colour, would blush if she was caught in some misdemeanour or other such as kicking the suckling calf away from her udders, or having to be fetched from the farthest corner of the meadow at tea-time, she having decided in her own stupid mind that it wasn't the calf's tea-time yet and she wasn't having her tea for master, calf or anybody else. On being routed out of her comfortable corner, the old fool would definitely blush. Both Ray and I were convinced of it.

As luck would have it, the departure from the Hill Farm wasn't to be the end of my adventures in the realm of agriculture, although what followed was very different from the stock rearing Ray and I had enjoyed. We were very excited when we heard that the farm down the lane from us had been rented by a Mr Haylett, who was described as an agricultural engineer - that is, he owned two splendid steam traction engines, plus threshing machinery and other items of mechanical farming equipment. He and his family moved into the semi-detached house practically opposite the school, and it was a wonderful day when tremendous earth-shaking processions brought Mr Haylett's magnificent engines and all their appurtenances into the confines of the farm. I went down the road and watched open-eyed as all these marvels safely manipulated the gateway into the farm and ranged themselves up side by side in the open part of the compound.

I have never been 'backwards in coming forwards' when something of great interest about which I want to know more is put within my reach. The engines and all the rest of the machinery hadn't been in occupation of the farm premises for more than a day when I took it upon myself to introduce myself to the owner of all this richness. Mr Haylett received me with the same politeness that I had extended to him and took my hand as that of a blood brother. He asked my name, where I lived and all that I could tell him about my family. He told me all I wanted to know about himself, where he had come from and his interests, and then gave me the freedom of his possessions on the farm, which were considerable, and the run of his workshops.

Mr Haylett was one of the most remarkable and self-taught craftsmen I have ever met. He was a very clever blacksmith, an accomplished turner both in wood and metal, a competent carpenter and joiner and a first-class engineer. He and his son did all the running repairs on their machinery, traction engines and all. His patience was monumental. I never once heard him use a profane word, despite the many breakdowns and mishaps to his machinery he had to put right, sometimes almost working through the night to keep a promised threshing arrangement. Always with a cheerful smile and a word of welcome, he would carry on with whatever he was doing when I walked into the forge or the carpenter's shop, and would treat me as an intelligent grown-up and explain to me what he was doing and why, and, mirabile dictu, would ask my advice, which he would ponder seriously and, without any air of condescension, thank me for. What a man.

Once when a funeral had just passed down the lane and we were chattering together in the carpenter's shop, Mr Haylett told me his father had apprenticed him at the age of 14 or thereabouts to the village carpenter and undertaker, a very respected man and a good tradesman. On the first day of his apprenticeship, his master was taking a coffin which he had just made to receive its occupant, an old lady who had died in the village. They wrapped the coffin in a piece of black hessian, put it in the workshop handcart and trundled it down the road to the cottage that had been her home. The narrow stairway of the cottage being awkward to negotiate with the coffin, the master got a ladder and decided to put it in through the bedroom window. Mr Haylett told me that he had never seen a dead body before and wasn't feeling too happy about it. He had to help his master lift the body off the bed where it was lying to put it into the coffin, which further unnerved him. However, worse was to come, because when they got the body to the coffin, it just wouldn't go in, try as they might. According to Mr Haylett, in his broad Norfolk accent "It had just swolled up with all the gases during the night". Eventually, after trying for some time, the old carpenter said to young Haylett "Do you close that door, boy", pointing to the bedroom door, which stood ajar. Haylett did so, upon which, to his horror, the old undertaker produced a clasp knife, opened it and plunged it into the corpse. With a sigh of escaped gases, the body subsided into the coffin.

"That was enough for me", said Mr Haylett. "I gave one yell, dived for the bedroom window, went down that there ladder in about two steps and ran for home as if the dogs were after me". He told me that he wouldn't tell his parents what had happened for fear of getting the old carpenter into trouble, but he flatly refused to go near that carpenter's shop again. His father took it that the boy was squeamish about corpses and found him another master to take him on. I can see Mr Haylett now, chisel in hand, telling me that story of his boyhood.

Mr Haylett and his men worked very hard, especially in the threshing season. One would be wakened at 5.30 am to hear the engine chuffing out from the farmyard gate. There was one thing that always puzzled me; the width of the gateway. Why did so tidy-minded and careful a man as Mr Haylett go through all the bother and trouble each time he took his machinery out of negotiating that narrow gate into the lane when it could so easily have been widened? The lane was very narrow and the gate was even narrower, so the engine and its two trailers, drum and elevator, could never make the turn into the lane in one go. Always, the drum and elevator had to be edged out with chains and wire and the men had to hang on to the draw bar of the drum or elevator to keep it from knocking down the gatepost. Finally, after all the backing and filling was over, the procession would head up the hill past the school en route to its next threshing date.

During the off season from threshing, Mr Haylett would refit and paint his engines and equipment. Sometimes he would put up a saw bench and saw planks for the village carpenter. I remember once getting roped in on a modification to one of the engines. Mr Haylett had decided that a drain hole had to be bored through the bottom of the casting which carried the slider mechanism of the engine (for those ignorant of these things, the slider mechanism is a large and clumsy bit of machinery that performs the same function as the timing mechanism on the internal combustion engine). It was going to be a very awkward job. One couldn't get an ordinary hand-drill to it as there wasn't room enough either in the slide path itself or from underneath, where there was less than six inches clearance between the bottom of the casting and the top of the boiler casing. Mr Haylett pondered this problem for a very long time, thinking out loud as he did so.

"There must be a way" he kept muttering. "It'll show itself if I keep looking long enough." And he would walk slowly back into the forge, me trailing at his heels, offering my feeble suggestions.

It was, in fact, something I said which produced the 'Eureka' (had he known the word) from Mr Haylett. He clapped me on the shoulder, exclaiming in his huge voice that he had found the solution.

"Ah got it, ah got it, you're right boy, that'll do it, only you'll hatter help. Will you?" I said I'd do anything to help, if help I could, or words to that effect. Dropping everything else he was doing and enlisting my aid to fetch and carry, he enthusiastically started to erect a simple apparatus to do the job.

I wonder if I can explain this. I'll try. He got a piece of steel strip about six or seven feet long and fastened it at one end to an upright stake, which he drove firmly into the ground. The piece of steel passed under the spot where the drilling was to be done and then was fastened to an upright jack on the other side of the engine, which could be turned to thrust its end of the steel strip upwards. He bored a small hole into the centre of the strip immediately under where the drilling was to be made. Then he put the bottom of a boring bit into this hole, and the bite part of the bit was centred where it should be on the underside of the casting. A spanner with a long-handled ratchet arrangement was fastened to the bit, and all that was needed to make the apparatus work was somebody to work the handle backwards and forwards. It was as simple as that.

Mr Haylett asked me if I would mind sitting up there on top of a stepladder and working the ratchet for him. I said that I would be delighted. To be considered a fit person actually to work on one of the traction engines was the height of glory to me, and I enthusiastically set to work.

I had a half-inch thickness of cast steel to bore through. It took me all day and cost me a pair of very sore shoulders, but I did it. I got my reward from the warm thanks of Mr Haylett whose tribute of, "Well done, couldn't a done it better myself!" was all I needed. Ever afterwards, I considered that particular engine to be my own special possession. The whole operation was the highlight of my young life. I have never been in the slightest degree mechanically minded, but there was deep satisfaction in what I had done.

I longed to be allowed to drive one of the engines, but that was forbidden, and one could see why. I was much too small to manipulate the large lever of the reverse mechanism, which had to be worked at the same time as the regulator. This was, so I gathered, to get the piston to the right place to get the full thrust from the steam. I was allowed once, in an emergency, to stop the engine. Mark you it was standing still at the time and was acting as the power unit to drive a saw bench, where some timber was being cut for one of the local boatyards. Something went a bit amiss at the saw bench. Mr Haylett, who was at that end of the proceedings, yelled, "Stop the engine!" at the top of his voice. I was the only one on the engine at the time, and having watched hundreds of times, I knew what to do and closed the regulator, thus bringing everything to a full stop. I got full marks for that, but I was still never allowed to start it.

Mr Haylett was a deeply devout man, but I could never fathom what particular denomination, if any, of the Christian faith he favoured. He used to come to Wroxham church on occasions, usually in the evenings, and always in great voice and trim at Harvest Thanksgiving. He used to tell me that he didn't care for our hymnal, the Ancient and Modern. "Them hymns are all very well but there ain't no 'goo' about them" he said.

He was very fond of a hymn-singing session, and on Sunday evenings we would often hear his lusty voice uplifted, bursting forth in such hardy favourites as Tell me the old, old story and Will your anchor hold in the storms of life, with Mrs Haylett working hard on their harmonium. Very frequently the Sutton family, who lived next door and were staunch Methodists, would join them. The Suttons were very musical too. Mr Haylett would tell me the next time we met what a wonderful evening they had enjoyed and say that I really must go over and join them some time and "have a good old sing".

To this day I love to go to a traction engine rally if one happens to be in the neighbourhood, if only to recapture the joys of a very happy period in my young life. The smell of a traction engine, something quite unmistakeable, and the sound of the chuff-chuff of the exhaust can transport me in a moment back to Mr Haylett's farm. I can hear his voice and feel his enthusiasm – he was always most enthusiastic in whatever he turned his hand to – and something of the magic of those halcyon days of early Wroxham come back to me.

I was obviously never destined to be a 'farmer's boy', but I look back with great feelings of thankfulness for the few years I spent in and around farms and farm workers. I learned a lesson then, which dear old Mr Haylett instilled into me. Can I explain it this way? The village was a village, and life was primitive. Sanitation was the old bucket system, and the buckets were always emptied and their contents dug deep into the householder's allotment or garden. Just after the Great War the County Council began to frown on this practice, so one of our number was selected to collect 'night soil' from the various privies in the village to be carted away and disposed of in a sanitary manner.

In our usual village way, it wasn't long before a nickname was fastened to this set up. It was known, quoting the old hymn chorus, as 'the pilgrim of the night', which meant that the hymn Hark, hark my soul, angelic sounds are swelling could never be sung without smirks and grins from both choir and congregation, almost to the point where it had to be on the 'not sung' list.

But I am not making my point, which was a remark made by Mr Haylett, and a profound one too, when he was discussing with me the introduction of the 'night soil' system. He hummed and hawed and thought, and then remarked to me that a lot of gardens and allotments would be the poorer for not having the contents of the buckets dug into them as had been done from time immemorial.

"It stands to reason you mustn't goo agin Nature" he said. "What Nature says is that what comes out o' the soil you've gotter put back into it, if you see what I mean'.

He was a simple but profound philosopher, Alfred J. Haylett, and I count myself very fortunate to have known him.

CHAPTER TWELVE

Play time

In one of the corners of the Infant Room in the school was a large wardrobe-type cupboard, which housed all the various bits and pieces of equipment necessary for the running of the kindergarten. On top of this cupboard were two large wicker baskets. To take the lid off one of these baskets was to be bombarded with the tang of at least a hundred and one mothballs. No self-respecting moth would ever dream of venturing within yards of those baskets.

They contained costumes, children-sized, which had been made and kept from the various concerts that Dadda and Mumma had organised for the school. The proceeds of these concerts always went towards providing every child in the school with a day at the seaside in the summer. The trip was eagerly looked forward to, and it was understood that we always went to Lowestoft, because, I suppose, the choir always had their outing to Great Yarmouth, and besides, Lowestoft, shall we say, was thought to be more genteel, more suited to our tender years. Also, it was smaller and there was less chance of any of us getting lost.

It was a tremendous event, this school outing to Lowestoft. If my memory serves me right, we usually went on a Saturday. In those days education was taken very seriously and it was very difficult indeed to get the education authorities to grant a day off for an outing. Possibly that is the reason why our generation can spell.

We were all instructed to be at the station at a certain hour. "Don't be there too soon and fall under a train or something. Be there at nine o' clock" we were told, and so a few minutes before nine one would see excited children coming along the various roads that met at the station. We each had to bring a tin mug for drinking purposes, which had to have the name of the owner clearly marked on it. Some of the younger fry had the mug fastened to a convenient buttonhole with a piece of tape or ribbon in order that it shouldn't be lost and that the unfortunate mug-loser should not subsequently die of thirst.

If the older ones were intending to bathe, their towel and costume had to be contained in a bag and not carried loose, again to avoid the risk of loss. It was all most carefully organised. We had each of us written out, copied from the blackboard, a list of instructions which we had taken home to mother. Our memories were not to be trusted with all the details. Dadda was a very wise man.

Mr Underhill the Stationmaster, a person of some consequence in the village, was on the platform to greet us, dressed, as was his wont on such an important occasion, in top hat and uniform frock coat. Mr Everett, the foreman porter, had the whole operation carefully planned. He knew exactly where our reserved carriage would pull up at the platform and we would be placed strategically on the right spot so that we could rapidly entrain and thus not cause any delays. They cared about punctuality on the railways too in those days.

Counted and mustered by our teachers, we waited excitedly for the arrival of our train. The knowledgeable ones among the older boys would be able to tell which signal would herald the great moment of arrival. We were always a well-behaved little mob and there were no stragglers. One or two mothers would come along for the day by the sea, but they would make their own arrangements and were not included in the official party.

The train pulled in and, directed by Mr Everett, came to a stop so that our reserved coach was exactly opposite us. Mr Everett having opened all the doors with his carriage key, we clambered in together with our teachers. Dadda remained on the platform till the last minute to make sure everybody was safely on board. When he eventually boarded the train Mr Everett locked every carriage door, finally giving Dadda a spare key so that he could open a door if necessary. We had all been directed to go to the lavatory before boarding, as the coach was not a 'corridor coach' and we had a fairly long journey ahead of us.

As the train pulled out from the station we cheered the stationmaster and Mr Everett. Mr Underhill took off his top hat and waved us away, shouting above the noise of the engine that he hoped we would have a good day. As the train gathered speed through the village of Wroxham, mums and dads who could spare the time would hang over the railway fence to wave to us.

When we arrived at Norwich Thorpe station there was further excited interest as our carriage, which was to take us all the way to Lowestoft, was detached from our first train and shunted round to be coupled to the Lowestoft train. There would be 20 minutes or so before the train left, so Dadda would get out and walk along the platform, asking if anybody 'wished to be excused' and, if so, 'it' was just *there*, and hurry up about it.

All safely back on the train, the guard blew his whistle, waved his green flag and we were off, with loud cheers, to Lowestoft. The journey down was fairly uneventful. The older children who had been on such trips before would count the stations at which we stopped and, as we got nearer to Lowestoft, excitement grew. When we arrived we were formed into a crocodile in our classes, with the older boys and girls carting the hampers containing our picnic dinner and tea, and set off for the beach.

It was always a great thrill if the Harbour Bridge happened to be open. The crocodile then had to stop while a tug perhaps towed a string of fishing smacks through to the fish desk. It was a great novelty to us to see the bridge slowly swing back into position, to hear the whistles of the bridge crew, to see through the windows of the engine-house the wheels of the bridge machinery slowly revolving and to watch the overhead wires of the tramways meet neatly with their opposites as the bridge settled with a little jump into its correct position. The road being open again, the crocodile set off once more to the beach by the pier. A central site was selected, and there our hampers and all our personal belongings could be left in safety.

A paddle, a swim, the making of sandcastles, the digging of a large hole in which to sit or, if funds allowed, a donkey ride, would occupy us until lunchtime. In the afternoon there was usually a Punch and Judy show to watch, or perhaps one of the teachers would call out, "Who wants to come on the pier with me and listen to the band and watch the ships?" A large party would muster with 'Miss' and they would spend a thrilling hour or so listening to the band and trying out the various machines on the pier.

The picnic lunch and tea were always a tremendous success. Everybody was always hungry. None of us had lashings of pocket money in those days, and we didn't see the fun of spending our few pennies on sweets and suchlike when food was provided for nothing. Our teachers would tell us to take careful note of everything, as we most certainly would have to write a composition on 'My Day at the Seaside' when we returned to school the following Monday.

And so a long and very happy day came to an end. The same careful organisation between Dadda and the railways brought us safely back to Wroxham, tired out, where a collection of mums and dads were there to meet us and hear ecstatic tales of a wonderful day by the sea. The children wouldn't forget, either, to give 'Three Cheers for the Teachers'. And so home by our various ways to bed and dreams.

But I intended to tell not of the treat but of the activities which made the treat possible, in other words, the School Concert. My parents had brought with them from Yorkshire the expertise of organising School Concerts – not a succession of rows of children doing their 'piece' or of some nervous child wavering through a solo followed by a few boys in white shorts and shirts demonstrating Swedish Drill, but a real live show. Our School Concerts were the real thing, a truly theatrical affair with costumes, scenery, make-up, lights and the lot. I have been involved in the amateur stage as a hobby all my life and these concerts were the beginnings of it. Dadda and Mumma used to stage children's operettas – *Sherwood Forest, Rip van Winkle, The Prince of the Mistletoe, The Dolls' Hospital* and many others. The School Concert actually consisted of two operettas, one for the Infant and Junior School produced by Mumma and her assistant with backing from Dadda, and then the solid piece of the evening, the operetta done by the senior children, which was quite something.

In the early days of these concerts the stage and all its fittings had to be rigged in the Middle Room of the school, and that must have been a monumental labour in itself. By the time I had grown old enough to partake in this play-acting, a Mr Curzon, a local builder and also something of a socialite (at least his sons were), had, as a speculative venture, built an 'Assembly Rooms' in the main street of the village. It had a stage, dressing rooms and all mod cons. I take off my hat to Mr Curzon and his sons. The Assembly Rooms weren't a Palais by any stretch of the imagination, but they did provide for the filling of a great need in the village. There was no village hall, only the schoolroom, and to rig that for a concert or, say, a whist drive, was a mammoth task, as nothing could be done till the children had finished at 4 pm. Then, at the end of the evening's entertainment, everything had to be squared off for school the following morning. So the Assembly Rooms were a boon and a blessing to the village.

The building has gone now, at least as the Assembly Rooms. It evidently didn't pay its way, which was a pity, and Mr Curzon had to sell up. He deserved better for his venture. Eventually it was bought by Mr Passmore, who lived 'Down the Avenue', and he presented it lock, stock and barrel to the Methodists, whose 'tin tabernacle' was about to fall about their ears. Later they couldn't cope with the overheads of the place and, since it had no endowments and they were small in number, they too had to part with it. It is now a dwelling place. A pity, it was wonderful for the village when it was in its heyday. We saw our first 'moving pictures' there, with the operator of the projector winding the handle of his machine standing in the middle gangway.

The School Concert that I can recall most clearly was the first in which I took an active part. I suppose I must have been about five years old. We juveniles were performing The Dolls' Hospital and the Seniors were presenting *The Prince of the Mistletoe*. For weeks and weeks we practised and rehearsed. We knew not only our own parts backwards but everybody else's too. We were all understudies of everything. I remember that our actions were very methodical, mechanical and precise. I was a 'tin soldier', one of a boxful, and I can remember my brothers and sisters weeping with laughter when they saw me in my costume. So far as I can remember it had no military significance about it at all, but appeared more like an enormous multi-coloured nightgown of no shape whatsoever. It draped on the ground all round, being much too long for me, and I had to walk very carefully, holding up the front like an old lady keeping her dress out of a puddle, while I grabbed, with the other free hand, the wooden rifle which was the only thing about me that marked me as a 'tin soldier'. Why I didn't fall flat on my face in our various drills and manoeuvres I just can't tell. I think that had I done so I would have been decapitated by Mumma, who was conducting operations from the piano, on the spot. But it didn't happen and we were a great success.

I can remember two highlights in the *Dolls' Hospital* apart from my Oscar performance as one of the 'tin soldiers'. Apples Coffin, then about six or seven years old, was the Apothecary in the operetta, and he brought the house down with his rendering of *Pills and potions, powders, lotions, I know how to mix*…. with a pestle and mortar nearly as large as himself containing flour which he liberally spread all over the stage in choking clouds as he pounded his pestle in time with the music. Old ladies in the audience were whooping with laughter. 'Apples' was a hit.

The other highlight was Stanley Stevenson, dressed as a sailor doll by his mother. He danced a most creditable Sailor's Hornpipe. Yet he hated every minute of it, and the expression of sheer misery on his face as he performed his convolutions had to be seen to be believed. Even the hisses of Mumma from the piano of "Smile, Stanley, Smile" made no change in his expression. He got roundly applauded all the way through, but each outburst of clapping only served to accentuate his misery. At our final curtain we were cheered to the echo, and then we little ones were allowed, in our costumes, rouge and all the rest of it, to creep down to the front and seat ourselves on a low bench to watch the 'big ones' perform.

Their show, *The Prince of the Mistletoe*, was an operetta about the Norse folk tale of Baldur, the Prince, and his age long battle with Loki, the wicked Troll. It was exceedingly well acted and produced. So impressed was I with this story and the very sentimental and haunting music that accompanied the unfolding of its plot and the excellent singing by the cast that I can remember most clearly both the music and the words of the opening chorus, when the four elements, earth, air, fire and water, introduced themselves, all bathed in an eerie light. Their song went,

We are the Elements, Elements four,
Four simple Elements, that and no more.

The costumes for the play, made by the sewing class at school under the guidance of Mumma, were most effective, as were the stage effects of thunder and lightning and all the rest of the marvels one would find in the Valhalla of the Gods. I can remember how, in the story, Prince Baldur was bewitched by the wicked Loki and looked likely to die. The only thing that could save his life was a tear-drop from Loki. He was captured and put into a cage (made by the boys under the direction of Mr Stevenson). Loki was cajoled and threatened, but no tear would he shed. We little ones were in an agony of apprehension lest Prince Baldur should die. I remember weeping buckets when a sad chorus sang "Baldur the prince is dead" to a most mournful dirge, and I just couldn't understand why Loki wasn't similarly affected. Then some character, I can't remember which it was, thought of tickling Loki, and at the same time the chorus sang to a treacly melody, "Just a little tear-drop to trickle from your eye, just a little tear-drop to show that grief is nigh" and Loki burst into tears. Baldur reappeared in all his beauty and the audience, moved to a man (and woman of course), stood and stamped and cheered as the curtain fell.

I think possibly the reason why this is so clear in my memory was because, as I have confessed in a previous chapter, I was very prone to floods of tears when I was a little 'tacker'. My brothers and sisters would often take advantage of this and tease me to try to get me out of the habit of bursting into tears at the slightest provocation. Marjorie, my eldest sister, when she saw tears about to be shed, would quietly sing "Just a little tear-drop to trickle from your eye", which would almost drive me demented. But the ridicule eventually cured me of what must have been to the rest of the family a most irritating and annoying habit.

The costume boxes were always raided at Christmas, or on some rainy day when dressing up became an interest. We and the Stevenson boys and girls, sometimes with the Chamberlains from our little post office, would don costumes and relive some of the stage successes of the school concerts.

During the Great War years the school concerts faded out, never to be revived, but Dadda found an outlet for his dramatic energies in our Scout plays and concerts. The old operettas faded into limbo and concerts became more of the variety type. I can remember one very vividly, the latter half of which was taken up by a Black and White Minstrel Show. Today I imagine it would just be called the Minstrel Show. Dadda's love of singing blossomed in this, because the main musical items in this show were the Scott Getty Plantation Songs, beautifully arranged and as beautifully sung. As a contrast to the knockabout comedy of Mr Interlocuter and Mr Bones these songs were lovely, and, at times, moved the audience almost to tears. It is most strange that in the revivals of minstrel shows these Scott Getty songs have never appeared.

The last of these concerts I can remember was put on in the Middle Room of the school, the Assembly Rooms having ceased as a concert hall. I remember appearing as a cook in a kitchen having great fun with a rolling-pin and some dough, to the huge delight of the audience.

But then came a great change in the life of drama in the village. The local medical fraternity and their friends decided to form a Dramatic Society. The leading light in this was our beloved local practitioner, Dr Aldred, a son of the parsonage and a most lovable personality. An inaugural meeting was held in the school. Dadda attended and was put on the committee.

A deal of enthusiasm was generated, and an opening show was planned. To produce this first show and to get the whole venture off on a sound basis of skill and theatrical expertise, they enlisted the help and advice of one known to be a most accomplished amateur actor and a first class producer, the vicar of the neighbouring parish of Worstead (famous for its magnificent 'wool' church and the fact that the village had given its name to the fabric known as 'worsted'). The Rev C W Kershaw introduced me and many of my contemporaries to the art of amateur acting. He certainly instilled into me a love of the stage, which I have never lost. He was a perfectionist, a great character actor and a very clever comedian.

The first show was to be a 'try-out' on the village, so they determined to keep their preliminary sights low, to do something within their known capabilities and to get the village on their side. To this end they decided on a double bill. The first of the programme was given over to the performance of a straight one-act comedy. This concerned a matrimonial bureau, and I can't for the life of me remember the name of that play. Dr Aldred played the male lead, much to the delight of members of his practice in the audience. To hear him mouth, "Miss Pop-Pop-Pop-Poppincourt" – the part required him to have a stammer – sent the folk out front into convulsions.

We would be well away if the second half of the double bill came up to scratch. It certainly did. It was one of the funniest shows, professional or amateur, I have ever seen, with Mr Kershaw providing the bulk of the outrageous comedy. I remember that my brother Ray and Stanley Stevenson, both about 14 years old, were involved in one of the comedy sequences. I was a most important 'man-in-the-wings' since I had to be 'spotlight man'. I was equipped with a brass car headlamp from Dr Aldred's Singer. It was lit by acetylene, which was generated in a gadget in the back. I had a large sheet of green glass and a large sheet of red glass for odd effects now and again. Incidentally, this show was put on in the school, and you can imagine the cramped quarters we worked in. The stage lighting was by acetylene gas generated by a large gadget in one of the lobbies outside and piped to wherever it was required. It stank the place out, because none of the joints were properly made. The tang of it flavoured the atmosphere of the school for weeks after the show.

The play was called *A Pantomime Rehearsal* and it purported to be the dress rehearsal of a pantomime being staged by a gang of enthusiasts like ourselves. It poked fun at the whole of the amateur stage movement. It was a musical, and a scratch orchestra was organised by a Mr Wightman, who had moved into the village at the end of the war and who was a talented musician. He was a very good organist and had taken over the post of organist in the village church. The orchestra, since there was no room for it in the front of the stage, had to be on the stage. What with pieces of spare scenery, a partitioned-off part where the men put on their costumes and were made up, bits of furniture, the space for the orchestra and all the rest of it, we were, to say the least of it, very cramped. However, it didn't matter much.

Talking of the orchestra, I must put in a story here of a most amusing incident. The fame of our show spread and we were asked to perform it in various other places, one of which was a fairly large hall in North Walsham. Mr Wightman thought he would like to have something a little more brash than a couple of violins, a cello and his piano, and thought it would help out the pantomime atmosphere if he had a trombone. Somebody volunteered the information that a Mr Temple, who lived in Hoveton St Peter, had a trombone. They had seen it hanging on the wall of his sitting room, so somebody approached Mr Temple, who said he would be delighted to come along to North Walsham with his trombone.

I wasn't there on this occasion, but Dadda was. He was speechless with laughter when he got home again. Apparently Mr Temple had turned up with his trombone and was given his seat in the orchestra, which was in front of the stage. There he sat, in the orchestra, with his music stand and his trombone. Every time the band struck up, he put his trombone to his lips, but he didn't blow one note from the beginning to the end of the show. Wightman was apopleptic, but even more so when he discovered that Mr Temple couldn't read a note of music, had never played the trombone in his life before and thought that they only wanted him there for show, which, as he was being paid for the outing, suited him down to the ground. The only person who didn't see the funny side of it was Mr Wightman. The trombone had belonged to Mr Temple's father and was regarded in the family almost as an heirloom. Any connection with music was purely coincidental.

What modern fire-fighting organisations would have said about our naked acetylene burners all over the place and the lack of any proper fire precautions over safety exits and that sort of thing I shudder to think, but the whole show was a tremendous success. Rarely have I heard such gargantuan laughter as issued from the throats of the denizens of Wroxham. From time to time it held up the show completely. I was lost for evermore to the stage. The tremendous enthusiasm of Mr Kershaw and his skill and brilliance as an actor captivated me. I hero-worshipped him, and he nobly responded. He taught me the rudiments of make-up and of stagecraft in general, and I remember him with great affection.

It was shortly after this particular show that a fete was arranged in the village to raise funds for the building of a proper village hall. The newly formed 'amateurs' were asked to put on a one-act play to be part of a concert that was to be held in a marquee on the evening of the fete. The committee decided to produce a wartime comedy called *In the Cellar*, which was concerned with a 'noble house' being accused of food hoarding. I landed the part of the pageboy, a cheeky young imp (type-casting, my family called it). The play opened with the pageboy, me, falling down some cellar steps to be caught by the butler, played by Dr Aldred.

We held our rehearsals in the kitchen of a local farmhouse, which was occupied by one of our leading members, a Mr J R E Draper, another wonderful character. In one corner of this kitchen was a flight of stairs leading to what used to be the servants' quarters of this old farmhouse. In fact, the whole setup might have been designed for our rehearsal's benefit.

The first rehearsal proved disastrous for me. True to stage directions, and having been taught by Mr Kershaw how to fall realistically, I launched myself down, to be caught at the bottom by the butler, Dr Aldred – and caught I certainly was. His wrist smashed right across my mouth, and with one resounding crack knocked my four front teeth clean out. The cast were terribly worried and upset about it, but I was quite unperturbed. In fact the only thing that scared me was that I might lose my part in the play. However Mr Kershaw assured me that I had sealed myself in the part for good and all. I looked far more the cheeky Albert minus four front teeth than I had done with a regular set of incisors.

Dadda wasn't best pleased at having to foot the bill for a top plate for my mouth at the early age of fourteen but the play was a great success. By a strange quirk of circumstance, some ten years later I played the part of Will Shakespeare in the play of that name by Clemence Dane. It was the Commemoration Play put on that year at King's College, London, when I was reading theology there. On the first night of this play, having to deliver a full-blooded speech on stage with plenty of vigour, I blew my little four-teeth plate clean out of my mouth on to the stage. Fortunately it was during the closing lines of the speech, and though my fellow players saw it they managed to control their mirth. I was able to drop a cloth I was holding on to the stage over the plate, recover it and get it back into my mouth without the audience being aware of what had happened. But for a moment or two, I was in a rare state of panic. A gap-mouthed Will Shakespeare would have taken some swallowing.

The Society, having tasted the delights of the stage, really launched out now into a full programme of productions. A new wooden hall was constructed 'down the bridge'; well-equipped with stage, dressing rooms and all things necessary, and there we put on our winter season of shows. I managed juvenile parts in quite a number of them. It was grand to be entrusted with our house key and to walk back through the village, sometimes from quite a distance, since we rehearsed quite a lot in people's houses very late at night. On half days from school, Dr Aldred, who had an extensive practice spreading over a very large area and was a very busy man, would collect me from my home in his car and we would drive round the countryside visiting his patients, me alongside him in his car helping him to learn his lines.

We had a great run of successes, but I think the greatest of them was the society thriller *Grumpy*, the name part of which had been created by the late Mr Cyril Maude. Mr Kershaw (who always appeared in the programme as C Shaw), was superb as Grumpy and we were delighted and very flattered when the Theatre Royal in Norwich, having been let down by a booking, offered us a week there. Half the week was devoted to *Grumpy* and the other half to a thriller, something like the old play *Diplomacy*.

I had a walk-on part in *Grumpy* with a couple or so lines to say. I remember telling my English master at the City of Norwich School about this; he was quite excited about it. He had heard of the Wroxham Amateurs and had often desired to see their work. He, by the way, was a founder member of the old Maddermarket Theatre Company and was devoted to the stage. He came to see the show and told me the next morning that he had very much enjoyed it but "wished he had seen more of Davies".

That week backstage at the Theatre Royal was wonderful. To watch the skill of the scene shifters and the whole technique of professional theatre was an eye-opener, except on the Friday night when some of the stage-hands got paid and went to the local, and forgot to be back in time for the curtain after one of the scenes. I remember Mr Kershaw had to remember very quickly that he was a parson, otherwise he would have blotted his copybook for good and all if he had said all he wanted to say to the stage manager of the Theatre Royal.

In an earlier chapter I mentioned a lady who lived 'Down the Avenue' called Miss Agnes Gardner King. During the years of the Great War, Miss King got most interested in relief work for the people of the Balkans, particularly the Serbians, and she used to run sales and suchlike to raise funds for them. We had noticed that from time to time she would be accompanied to church by four young people, two boys and two girls. It eventually trickled down to us through the grapevine that these young people were her nephews and nieces, that their name was MacDonald and that they were the children of Ramsay MacDonald, the Scottish politician. It wasn't a name that meant much to us although, of course, we had heard of him through the newspapers. However, on one of the visits of these young people, Miss King decided to have an invitation concert in her house, where there was a lounge quite big enough for the purpose with a raised dais big enough to be called a stage. Talent in the village was tapped, and the church choir – I have already told you about our singing – was included in the performance to sing some part songs. The grand *pièce de résistance* of the concert was to be a performance of some scenes from *Macbeth*, to be played by the young MacDonalds. I remember that Malcolm Macdonald played Macbeth and the elder of his two sisters Lady Macbeth. That was the first time I ever saw Shakespeare performed, and I can still hear Malcolm MacDonald saying in broad Scots, "Is this a dagger that I see before me?". I have often wondered whether he remembered that particular concert. There was, too, a lady who whistled (a 'siffleur' she was described in the programme) and I believe a piano accompaniment. She whistled the famous *Whistler and his dog*.

Later, after the Great War was over and we had raised the money for our Village Hall at Wroxham (you may remember I lost my four front teeth in one of those endeavours), the elder MacDonald, Alastair, who was an architect, was the designer.

Parson and actor, you know, go hand in hand. Each has to possess some quality of the other and, as I have remarked, the stagecraft learned in my early years in Wroxham, like so many other things, has had a lasting influence in my life. One more remembrance surges through, not one of boyhood but from much later in life, yet the roots were established in the Wroxham of my youth.

In the August of 1939, before the actual declaration of war, I left Portsmouth in HMS *Despatch*, a 'brought-back' light cruiser, a vintage piece from 'up the trot'. We were en route for our war station, which, we had been led to believe, was Cape Town. For various reasons we never got there, for after the outbreak of war, rumour had it that a pocket battleship of the German Navy was in the South Atlantic. Our puny armaments would have been no match for the superior firepower of that ship, so we were detached from our convoy duties and shot off westwards across the Atlantic to Bermuda.

There we docked, and on completion of that exercise, we found ourselves bound for the Panama Canal via Jamaica. This was in early November. We then went through the canal into the Pacific, had a quick glance at the Galapagos Islands and steamed slowly down the west coast of South America, just out of sight of land, hoping that some of the German merchantmen bottled up in the South American ports would try to make a break for home and give us a chance of a prize or so.

Isolation could not have been more complete. No other RN ship was in those waters at that time. All ports south of the Equator were neutral, which meant that food and fuel were problems to the command, since, by the rules of war, ships of belligerent nations could only be supplied with that amount of food and fuel such as would get them safely at economic speed to the nearest friendly base.

In addition to that hazard, all our mails had gone to South Africa, our original war station. Radio communication with the UK was difficult, if not impossible, because of the blanketing effect of the high Andes ranges. Apart from a number of officers and a few 'key ratings', the greater percentage of the ship's company were RNVR, mostly Scotsmen from the Clyde, Campbelltown and the Isles. When we mobilised, with Munich in mind, I don't think any of us had any idea that the war would last longer than a few months or that accordingly we wouldn't be home again for a very long time. Actually, we quite expected to be back in our home port for Christmas.

We had little or no idea of what was happening at home – no mails to tell us what was going on on the home front or how our folk were faring, and very little opportunity of getting letters home either. Morale was not exactly at rock bottom, but it wasn't all that high. As Ship's Chaplain I would sit in my cabin evening after evening listening to the outpourings of various lonely souls, who knew of course that there was nothing I could do except listen, and put in a comforting word where I could. Remember, I was a regular, they were volunteers. My home arrangements were such as every regular makes for his life of enforced separation, which he and his family accept as the exigencies of the service. The RNVR chap, not thinking long term, had not had time to get his home affairs sorted out before sailing, and in many cases just didn't know what was happening, nor what he could do about it. If ever a modern ship's company felt like the old timers who circumnavigated the globe with Drake with no home connections, we felt at one with them.

Well, there we were, lazing along, just out of sight of land, hoping that we might justify our existence by catching a 'Jerry' ship alive as it tried to make its way home to Germany. We did catch one, and we sent it with a prize crew on board through the Panama Canal on Christmas Day 1939, the White Ensign flying above the Swastika.

But conditions on board were not improving. A number of RN ships about that time were boasting about having been at sea for many days without any let-up. I'm sure we must have qualified somewhere along the line, although I never heard of our being mentioned. I have just been looking through some old papers of those early days of the war, among which I found this record from a documentary programme I had arranged on board. It reads: "Up to December 31st 1939, from the outbreak of war, out of 119 days, we had done 106 steaming and not a man in the ship, from Commodore downwards, had slept out of the ship from August 15th 1939 – February 28th 1940. We had no serious sickness, one major breakdown (steering) repaired at sea. We got our 1939 Christmas mails at Easter 1940 and our Christmas parcel mail at Whitsun 1940."

It was after a particularly difficult day; a stray BBC broadcast had been heard on our ship's radio and we learned of the bombing at home. We were all very worried. I had more visitors in my cabin than I care to remember. It would be late in November 1939. That evening I went to have a natter with the Commodore. My object was to ask if he had any plans for Christmas – a stupid question under the circumstances. What plans could there be? Neutral ports, German agents watching every move and no chance or opportunity for leave, but I felt I had to tell him, as if he didn't already know, what the chaps were thinking. Besides, the Commodore had his own problems, not the least of which was the heavy burden of some 700 or so souls under his command and care. He opened his heart to me that evening, just as would a lonely sailor, and I almost had to comfort him in the same way.

Christmas was a problem which he recognised. "Wait a minute Padre", he said. "Let's consult the Pilot (Navigating Officer) and see what suggestions he has." So the Pilot was duly fetched in from the chart room.

"The Padre has a problem about Christmas, Pilot," he said, "Do you have you any ideas?"

"Well, as a matter of fact Sir" said the Pilot, "I had thought about a break if we could manage one.".

"Any particular place in mind?"

"Well, what about Port Yates, Sir?"

Down to the southward on that lonely west coast, there is an archipelago of broken coastline with deep indentations, many islands and hidden bays and anchorages. We had poked our noses in there earlier, in our search for German shipping. One of the places we had visited, where a small party had also landed, was an anchorage deep in the islands called, on the charts, Port Yates. It must have been an old whaling station (I'm guessing here), or so we thought, because we had found the skeleton of a whale. I remember that Joe Britton, Commodore's Secretary, had come off with part of the whale's backbone, which he thought might make a novelty seat. He kept it for a while in the Commodore's office until Bill Collyer, the Chief, complained of the smell. What happened to it after that I wouldn't know.

We also found a cross over an old grave mound. Any inscription had long since been weathered away. What a lonely place to die and be buried, we thought. There were no other signs of human habitation; the whale bones and the grave were the only signs that man had ever been there, with, of course, the name of the anchorage, Port Yates.

It was summer in those latitudes, and the surrounding moorland was covered with acres upon acres of bilberries, or blaeberries, call them what you will. The chaps gathered these and eked out our Spartan menus with pies and tarts and what-have-you. After all, it was fresh fruit, and we hadn't seen much of that. Its tartness and our hunger for it gave us a rare spate of bellyaches. The Doctor said that there was no harm in that. In fact he thought the healthy change of diet would have done us good.

Port Yates was some miles in from the open Pacific, and the Pilot thought that we might safely hide ourselves there for two or three days over the Christmas period. Remember that not a man of us from the Commodore downwards had spent one night out of the ship since mid August. So far as we knew, there was no human habitation for miles around.

But what to do for Christmas? That was the question. The Commodore decided that we would get permission to put into Valparaiso in Chile and stock up as best we could with Christmas fare. I remember that at that time we had run out of cigarettes on board and chaps were actually smoking their ration of Pusser's tobacco in cigarettes made out of an outer covering of RN lavatory paper.

Anyway, after stocking up as best we could with Christmas goodies, we thought we might pay a call on Juan Fernandez, that remarkable extinct volcano-crater island off the coast of Chile. It is the home waters for the most remarkable lobsters and shoals of rock-cod, which almost jumped on board, so eager did they appear to be caught. A survivor from the German cruiser *Dresden*, sunk there in the First World War, still lived on the island. He watched us from a distance.

The Pilot remarked to me as we leaned over the guardrails watching the scene, and an interesting scene it was too. Never have I seen such remarkable prowess in horsemanship as was demonstrated by children about three or four years old on pony back with their mounts clambering up and down almost impossible terrain. The Pilot remarked to me, "It's supposed to be Robinson Crusoe's island, you know". This was certainly news to me, but it sparked off a train of thought. Why not a pantomime for Christmas? Why not *Robinson Crusoe*?

It was still a month or more to Christmas, and all the expertise of do-it-yourself entertainment, the seeds of which had been planted in me by Dadda in far off Wroxham so long ago, came surging into my mind. I dashed in to see the Commodore (what a long-suffering man he was) and asked permission to stage a pantomime. He thought I'd gone barmy, but agreed. However he warned me that the exigencies of the service might make it impossible at the last minute to put it on. "I give it my blessing," he said. "See the Commander, and good luck go with you'.

I got together one or two keen officers and a number of the rest of the ship's company and we set to work to make our plans. Costumes – where were they to be obtained? The Senior Engineer immediately said, "What about the rag-bags? There's some of those in the Engineer's store that haven't been touched since we left England. You might find something amongst that lot".

To the uninitiated I had better explain that the engineering world on board were supplied with bags of rags to be used as 'wipers-up' in the engine rooms. We explored these sacks of rags and unearthed treasures untold, in the shape of old women's jumpers, pyjamas and nightgowns, dresses of all kinds and shapes, stockings, drawers, petticoats and what-have-you. One of the Leading bunting-tossers (signalmen) was a dab hand with the sewing machine, and he furbished up the most marvellous selection of costumes. I wrote a script with every overtone of topical illusion. I used for tunes the old melodies I had known as a boy, plus one or two of the modern catchy tunes. Enthusiasm bubbled over. We had a small Royal Marines band on board with a most cooperative and helpful bandmaster. He orchestrated and arranged the music for a small orchestra consisting of my portable 'squeeze-box' (folding harmonium, destroyer type), a couple or so fiddles, a clarinet, a cornet and drums.

The days slid by as we slowly steamed south, and we rehearsed as best we could. The only place we could use as a rehearsal space was the Engineer Artificers' workshop, a space full of lathes and other mysterious pieces of machinery. It was difficult, and hot, but there was nowhere else suitable. The First Lieutenant promised that for the actual show he would rig up some sort of a stage on the quarterdeck under the awning, but that we wouldn't get that until the actual afternoon of the show, which was to be staged during the dogwatches on Boxing Day.

The show turned out to be a tremendous success. There was a hirsute and wild-looking Fairy Queen in a ballet skirt fringed round the top of two thin bony-looking and hairy legs, a fiendish Demon King (one of the RM Colour Sergeants), myself as the Dame and various other officers and ratings taking the other parts and acting as Chorus. The quarterdeck was crowded – every man that could be spared from essential duties was there. The Commodore, surrounded by his heads of department, occupied an armchair in the centre of the front row. The costumes were also a tremendous success and I have always carried theatrical make-up around with me, so that side was taken care of.

There wasn't a dull moment. One of the most successful numbers was a song reflecting the state of the larder of the ship at that time. A great standby for meals on board was a variation on the theme of tinned 'Herrings in Tomato Sauce' known on board as 'errins in'. My song, put over by a young Clydesider with a tremendous sense of humour and wonderful stagecraft, went to the tune of *Poor Old Joe* and the refrain, which was plugged as an audience participation number went:

Nae Nutty, nae Nutty, it's a shame and it's a sin:
We hear the mournful mess-man moanin', 'errins in

'Nutty', I hasten to explain, is still the sailor's word for any kind of chocolates or sweets. We had run out on board several times. 'Nae Nutty meant that NAAFI on board had 'no sweets'. The audience yelled it out in true style, the Commodore lifting his voice with the rest of us. But it was the final number that literally brought the house down. It was a very sentimental number, which went to the tune, very popular at the beginning of the war, There'll always be an England'. The refrain went:

Good luck to those in England, good luck to those at home,
Good luck to every sailorman that on the seas doth roam
Good luck to every sweetheart, good luck to every wife,
Good luck to every boy and girl who're starting out in life.

Unfortunately I haven't a copy of the rest of the words, but they were in the same sentimental vein. The Demon King led the singing and I don't think, as the final curtain was pulled, that there was a dry eye either on stage or in the audience. There was silence for a moment, then pandemonium broke out. I have never known such a demonstration of sheer exuberance, relief and appreciation as burst forth. There were yells and cheers as the curtains opened again and I remember seeing the Commodore, normally a dour and silent man, sitting on the back of his armchair, tears streaming down his face, waving and yelling with the best of them. No West End playwright could ever have experienced such an ovation as we did on the first and last night of *Robinson Crusoe*, a pantomime staged as far south, I should think, as any that has ever been produced.

Remember the lads had had no cinema (we hadn't such a thing on board), no UK radio (we couldn't get it), and no kind of entertainment except for such dogwatch activities as I could organise on board in the evenings.

The stage and fittings were pulled down at once, and the lads all went below to change. I thanked the rigging crew and then made my way across the quarterdeck to my cabin. As I passed the door of the Commodore's day cabin, which opened on the quarterdeck, he shot out and seizing me by the hand, pumped it up and down, stuck a large gin in my hand and thanked me effusively.

"Thank you a thousand times Padre," he said. "You've done something for me and for this ship's company, which you will find will have made a tremendous difference to our lives from now on. I can't tell you how grateful I am to all of you."

And then a surprise. "I know it isn't normally done" (and it certainly wasn't done in those days) "but will you get hold of every member of your team, players and back-stage crew, and bring them to the wardroom, just as they are, to have a drink with me? I've fixed it with the Commander. Off you go, and mind you get 'em all." I soon rounded them all up and brought them along to the Wardroom.

That show marked for me a high spot in my life. It shines down the years like a beacon, and I am sure that the whole affair stemmed from those happy learning days of my childhood in Wroxham, where we were taught to make our own amusements and where we could quite well have coined that telling phrase "Do your own thing".

Footnote: HMS Despatch had a long and isolated deployment. The pantomime was one of several events organised by the Padre and was a great boost to morale among the ship's company. The Reverend Clifford Davies was awarded his OBE (Military) for his tour in Despatch.

CHAPTER THIRTEEN

The passing of the wherrymen

I march across great waters like a queen,
In whom so many wisdoms helped to make;
Over the uncruddled billows of seas green
I blanch the bubbles highway of my wake.

The title of this chapter may sound like a trumpet call of doom. In fact my intention is to pay tribute to the community of watermen, those plying their trade on the rivers of Norfolk and Suffolk who vanished during the first half of the 20th century. Conservation, as we now know that word, came too late for them to achieve survival.

The rivers of the Eastern Counties had for years been the main roads for trade and the transport of heavy and bulky cargoes. My own river, the Bure, rises above Aylsham, some miles upstream from Wroxham. From Aylsham to Coltishall it was a canal, with locks which made it navigable for the wherries. Possibly Anne Boleyn, that tragic Queen, may have played on its banks, since Blickling Hall, the home of her family, is close by Aylsham.

The Bure joins the sea at Great Yarmouth, some 27 miles by river from Wroxham Bridge. Before the First World War, great black trading wherries plied to and from Aylsham and Great Yarmouth. These massive sailing boats passed by our Caen Meadow at all times of the year, up the slow and sluggish Bure to Coltishall, Buxton Lammas or Aylsham, or downstream towards Wroxham Bridge and thence to Yarmouth. The cargoes they carried in their capacious holds were many and various; gravel and marl for the roads, timber from the Scandinavian ships that called at Great Yarmouth, malt and barley for the breweries, bricks, coal, cheap tin trays - in fact they would carry anything that came their way.

The wherries were remarkable craft, built by remarkable craftsmen. They were constructed by the eye - 'Let your eye be your guide', was the trade motto of the wherry builders. I remember very vividly one of the Pitcher family (great wherrymen), Fred, who had worked on wherry building. It was Fred who gave me the old wherrybuilder's motto quoted above. I recall watching him doing a job of carpentry on an old boat belonging to Mr Lawrence, stationmaster at Wroxham at the time. I remarked to Fred that he didn't appear to work as did a normal boat builder, with carefully drawn plans and templates to hand. "Yew don't want old templates," said Fred. "Let your eye be your guide." Fred built some remarkably trim boats in his day.

But to return to the wherries – they were peculiar to Norfolk and Suffolk, constructed to navigate the slow, winding rivers of these counties. They were shallow drafted and had one sail only, a large black rectangle of very coarse canvas, gaff-rigged at the top and free at the base, with a tremendously strong tackle of sheet with pulleys to match to manoeuvre it when under sail. This sail was very heavy and usually required the combined strength of the skipper and his mate to hoist it. The clacketing of the ratchet on the windlass was a familiar sound to us as the wherries approached or departed from the two bridges, rail and road, that crossed the river at Wroxham Mill.

There were rows of reefing cords on these sails, but rarely did I see them in use. Usually, if there appeared to be too much wind for the full sail, the skipper would drop the peek, a most ungainly-looking and dangerous-seeming action, but it always appeared to work all right, without danger to life and limb. On wild windy days, with a gale roaring over our shallow valley from the north west, I can see in my mind's eye two or three of these wonderful craft tearing down the river along the Caen Meadow, with foaming white 'bones in their teeth' and thin wisps of smoke blowing from the little chimney above the cabin aft, where the crew lived. The skipper would be smoking his pipe, one hand on the great tiller bar, the other holding the sheet, while his mate would be head and shoulders above the opening of the small cabin, passing the time of the day, not in the least perturbed at the wildness of the elements.

The Broadland rivers are shallow and never more than 20 or 30 yards wide. The draft in the upper waters never exceeded eight or 10 feet, and that in the midstream. The wherries could sail closer to the wind than any craft I have ever known. It almost appeared at times that they could sail straight into the wind, which of course is absurd; but, aided by the quant, a long pole with a shoulder butt at one end and a forked mud fluke at the other, they processed in stately fashion up the short reaches of the rivers, making astonishingly fast progress.

I am talking now of the first decade of this century. The great Norfolk Flood of 1912 altered everything as far as the Bure was concerned. Coltishall lock and bridge went. It became impossible to get a wherry, or any other boat for that matter, up the river-canal beyond Coltishall, so the upper reaches of the river leading to Aylsham were closed for all time to through wherry traffic and the sad decline of the era of water transport as a trade route set in.

The crewmen of the wherries were a race apart. Some of their sons and daughters went to my father's school and were my contemporaries there. Through generations of men 'quanting' - walking a narrow plankway down either side of the craft to navigate the vessel down awkward reaches with a contrary wind blowing – the wherrymen seemed to have developed remarkably small and dainty feet. Even on land they had a marked habit of very precise and tidy walking, placing one foot exactly in front of the other foot almost as if they were still treading that narrow footpath along the side of the wherry. One could always recognise a wherryman and his children by their tiny, dainty feet and their tidy walk.

They were wonderful craftsmen too. I remember seeing Nat Bircham (the Birchams were a great wherry family) perform a feat of navigation I wouldn't have believed had I not seen it. As he rounded the bend by Powles' boatyard in Wroxham, turning into the Bridge reach, he dropped the mainsail and the mast single-handed. Keeping the way on his craft, he next shot the road bridge without touching it and continued on along the reach up the Railway Viaduct. He shot that, then raised the mast and sail and carried on with the craft up to Belaugh.

It is worthwhile here to recall some of these wherrymen's names, the names of families who are still in the Wroxham district: the Birchams, Presses, Pitchers, Webbs, Collins, Kerrisons and Gedges. I can see all these men in my mind's eye. They had their own very high codes of conduct and were weatherwise to a degree. When wind and tide were against them they would tie up at the Mill Staithe or by the Granary at Wroxham Bridge, and I can remember as a small boy seeing some 12 or 14 of these handsome craft tied up along the staithe there waiting for a favourable wind to waft them down to Great Yarmouth. Lovely names those boats had too – *Chloe, Harvester, Dragon, Golden Gleaner, Heather, White Heather* and *Lady Violet*, to name but a few.

Many are the stories circulating through the Broadland about the characters and deeds of the wherrymen. One such comes to mind. It tells of two brothers well known up and down the river. For years two brothers crewed a particular wherry. For the sake of clarity, I will call them Jimmy and Jack. They were both of an age, within a couple or so years, and at the time of which I am writing I should say they were in their late forties. They were watermen to their fingertips, but thoroughly dissimilar in every other respect, or so I was told.

Jimmy, at some time or other in his career, had been 'saved', perhaps at the Mission to the Deep Sea Fishermen in Great Yarmouth or in the small Bethel in the village of Hoveton St John close by Wroxham Bridge. That Hoveton Bethel is still there and its little band of worshippers have withstood all the blandishments and offers made to them by local big stores to buy their building out. As sturdy and independent as its congregation, the little 'tin tabernacle' still survives, with the towering blocks of Roy's stores all around it. It bears mute witness to the ruggedness of the faith as practised by Jimmy and his fellow believers.

Jimmy was often to be seen on Sunday evenings in the summer testifying at the centre of a circle of 'believers', tears streaming down his cheeks. The service was held in the open air. Brethren would come from the villages around, usually along with a few instrumentalists with their cornets, euphoniums and a drum and a few tambourines from the Salvation Army contingent at Coltishall. They would lift up their voices in the choruses, and visitors and villagers alike assembled on the Granary Staithe would listen and perhaps join in. If it happened to be one of those weekends when a number of wherries were moored at the Mill, quite a number of Jimmy's fellow wherrymen would join him.

His brother Jack was a roisterer, but not a belligerent or a troublesome one; he was never a nuisance to anybody, though he liked his pint and the convivial company of his fellows. They would enjoy a get-together on those rare occasions when the vagaries of wind and tide had caused a foregathering of the craft and their crews, say at Wroxham Bridge, Horning Ferry or the Anchor at Coltishall.

I have heard tales of Jimmy and Jack with a deal of laughter-cum-admiration at Yarmouth, Norwich, Beccles, my own native Wroxham and even as far afield as Ipswich, where, once on a Sunday evening in a beerhouse frequented by the skippers of London barges, it was discovered that I haled from Broadland. One of those present asked me if I had ever met Jimmy and Jack, the famous Broadland wherrymen brothers. Needless to say, I had free beer for the rest of the evening.

There was an occasion when, so I've been told, the two brothers were bringing their wherry upstream against wind and tide, a wearisome job, and they were sharing the tedium. One was quanting, the other seeing to the tiller and sail, the craft making slow progress. The evening was wearing on and the thirst was upon Jack. As the progress of the wherry got slower and slower, he saw his evening pint fading rapidly. Jack bided his time until the wherry got above St Benet's Abbey and the mouth of the Ant. He arranged at that moment for Jimmy to take over the quanting and then, by a bit of subtle manipulation of sail and tiller, brought the craft close into the right bank. Then, having fastened the main sheet to its cleat, he quietly stepped ashore before Jimmy could stop him and legged it for all he was worth over the marshes, taking the odd dyke in his stride, hell-bent on his pint at the

Ferry Inn at Horning. As the crow flies from the mouth of the Ant, that isn't too far for a thirsty wherryman.

Poor Jimmy was left alone. Jack arrived in a muck sweat at the Ferry Inn and fortified himself with a succession of pints. His thirst satiated, he waited on the staithe in front of the inn for wherry and brother to come down the reach. Then he quietly stepped back on board to take the quant from Jimmy, and they peacefully pursued their way upstream.

Jimmy would be heard fervently petitioning the Almighty for an act of conversion on his brother, that he might be saved from the error of his ways, but Christian forbearance would stifle any resentment or vituperation. They were never heard to quarrel.

So far as my memory serves me, the best story of these two brothers concerns a happening which brought near-disaster to themselves and their wherry in the harbour at Great Yarmouth. They had been on a run up to Norwich on the Yare to pick up a heavy cargo for transport to Coltishall. On the return trip they had the tricky task of judging the turn from the Yare into the Bure at the head of the harbour at Yarmouth. For some unknown reason they had misjudged the tide, which was not yet slack, as they thought. Instead of gracefully slipping under sail from the one stream into the other by kind permission of the slack water, they found the wherry seized by the current and whisked down Yarmouth Harbour towards the sea, yawing from side to side and twisting helplessly as it struck the eddies in the fast-ebbing tide.

I can remember hearing the scene described by an onlooker. The main danger was that the heavily-laden wherry might strike one of the piers of the old Haven Bridge, which in those days was a rare menace to navigation. This could have capsized the craft or badly holed it. There wasn't much time.

Helplessly they swirled and twisted downstream with the ebbing tide. It was said that Jimmy, the 'saved' one, put his trust in the Almighty ('the stilling of the storm'). Kneeling with arms outstretched on the foredeck, he prayed loud and earnestly to his Maker for divine assistance in their predicament. Phrases like "Peace! Be still!" alternated with snatches of "Eternal Father, strong to save" and "Will your anchor hold in the storm of life?".

In the sternsheets, Jack was dancing like a mad dervish. In the midst of the most bloodcurdling maledictions on the perversity of the river and its tides, to say nothing of the man who had compiled the tide tables, he was calling on all and sundry – "Don't stand there looking on like a bushel of half-wits, b***** well give us a hand!"

I was told that the wharfingers and other onlookers were thoroughly enjoying the spectacle, and proffering all kinds of advice. Then, as luck would have it, a motorboat which was in the vicinity saw the danger, and I suppose a chance of salvage money. Her skipper smartly got a line on board the wherry in the nick of time, brought her under control and towed her up to the Bure Yacht station, where she could safely wait for the flood tide to take her up the Bure.

A long argument then ensued as to which of the two had really saved the wherry. It lasted almost to the grave. Jimmy always maintained, as did his Brethren friends, that it was the intervention of the Almighty in answer to his prayers and choruses that brought them succour in the shape of the small tug, whereas Jack and his cronies insisted that his stentorian yells had activated the tug-skipper and saved the day; you pays your money and takes your choice. Whatever the outcome, the story served for many moons up and down the rivers on nights when wherrymen gathered in the riverside Broadland inns and told the tales of their craft.

Meditating on the above history, and in particular on the references to the Brethren, I remember once that I was walking with my family up Church Lane at Wroxham after Sunday evensong. The wind, what there was of it, was blowing gently from the north-east, and we could hear from time to time the distant sounds of the Salvationist's band playing choruses on the Granary Staithe. No doubt Jimmy and his fellow worshippers were offering their 'Evening Prayer'. Being a very small boy at the time, and feeling, I suppose, superior in the worship of the Establishment in which I had just taken part, I made some derogatory remark about the Brethren. Dadda quietly interrupted me

"We don't all worship God in the same way, Cliffy" he said. "There are many gates into the Kingdom of Heaven, and nobody has any monopoly over the one he uses. All people don't worship as we do, but it doesn't mean they are deprived of communion with God. It's the people who know nothing whatever of worship who need our thoughts and our help".

I felt myself justly rebuked, and filed the teaching at the back of my mind.

That conversation came home to me many years later. In the spring of 1937 I was on my first ship, the County Cruiser *HMS London*, in the Mediterranean, and we were tied up in Malta Grand Harbour. I had been on a bathing 'banyan' with some of the seaman boys and had been bitten by sandflies, as a result of which I had contracted a mild dose of dengue fever, a complaint which has a very depressive effect on the victim. I was confined to my cabin and my bunk and was feeling pretty low. It was a Sunday evening – my evening service had been cancelled and the captain had taken morning worship - and I was lying in my bunk turning things over in my mind. I had come to the conclusion that I wasn't a raving success as a Naval Chaplain, and that perhaps I had better write to the Chaplain of the Fleet offering my resignation, with the request that I might be permitted to return to the 'Church on the Beach'.

In the middle of this surge of self-pity, there came a soft knock at my cabin door. I called out "Come in", and there entered a very quiet-looking 'Sparker' Petty Officer whom I knew by the name of Holmes. I couldn't say that I knew him very well – the ship had only been in commission some three months – but I bade him welcome and offered him a cigarette, drawing attention to the fact that I was laid by the heels and therefore was neither mobile nor particularly bright. I said I would do what I could for him, thinking that it was some kind of need for compassion that had brought him along.

I asked him to sit down, which he did. He declined a cigarette, saying he didn't smoke, and then said that there was really nothing that I could do for him. Then with a shy smile he asked: "Is there anything I can do for you?"

Now this was a facer! What on earth did he mean? But almost as in answer to my unspoken thoughts he said, "Padre, if I was sick and in the Bay, you as my chaplain would come and visit me, I suppose?" I said that of course I would - it was part of my duty as a chaplain always to visit the sick. He then went on, "Well, since there is no other chaplain on board this ship, I suppose there is really no one to pay you that sort of a visit." I said that short of a chaplain coming in from some other ship in the Squadron that there was indeed no-one.

"So I thought" said Mr Holmes. "Well, I happen to be a member of the Christian Brethren. God has called me to pay you a sick visit. Do you mind?"

"Well, no," I said, wondering what was to come, and if I was about to be attacked by some religious fanatic — although I must say that Holmes didn't look a bit like that.

"No, I don't mind a bit, Mr Holmes" I said. "You just carry on!"

With that gentle smile still on his lips, he said "I would like to pay you the same sort of sick visit that I hope you might pay me were I laid by." Then, taking from his pocket a well-worn Bible, he read me the 23rd Psalm, beautifully and meaningfully. He talked to me gently on the subject of the Good Shepherd, and I will always remember his coming to the phrase "Thy rod and thy staff, they comfort me". As he talked I felt all my ills, worries and uncertainties seem to slip from my shoulders and a wonderful sense of peace and purpose seemed to possess me.

He finished what he had to say, offered a very simple and moving prayer, gave me a blessing and quietly left the cabin. I was too overcome even to say thank you or bid him goodbye. As he closed the cabin door I turned my face into my pillow and wept like a child — tears of thankfulness and relief. I fell into a peaceful sleep, which appeared, when I woke much later, to have banished my sickness and its accompanying black depression, together with all my fears and uncertainties. I did not write my letter of resignation to the Chaplain of the Fleet. I buckled down to the job in hand.

I have never forgotten that incident. Holmes was a tremendous source of strength to me in that ship for the rest of that commission. Some years later, during the Second World War, when I was serving with the Royal Marines at Lympstone in Devon, a Warrant Officer whom I knew to be of the Brethren quietly said to me: "I have heard from Brother Holmes. He knows you are serving here with me and has asked me to pray for you and help you."

I remembered my father's words on that long ago Sunday evening, that there are many gates into the Kingdom of Heaven, and for that wonderful saying of Tennyson that "more things are wrought by prayer than this world dreams of".

As I said earlier, the 1912 flood and the improvements in road communication, plus the growth of the pleasure craft on the Broads, put paid to the trading wherry and its devoted skippers. For some years a few hardier souls who refused to give in converted their craft in the summer months to serve the needs of the growing Broads cruising fraternity. Ernest Collins converted quite a few of their craft permanently, and beautifully fitted out they were. Miniature pianos were part of the furnishings of some of them, and I can well remember seeing one of these gracious craft with a happy crowd of holidaymakers on board, having brought up the piano from the state room below on to the forecastle to have a sing-song as they passed along the shores of the Caen Meadow.

As the yachting season only lasted about four months, it became more and more expensive to keep these great craft as paying propositions. They took up so much room in the boatyards and their maintenance costs were so heavy that eventually they were phased out. Gradually they disappeared from the Broadland scene, banished up creeks to rot away, or converted into coal barges or lighters for the quay-heading firms (those who drove stakes into the Broads mud to make staithes) or rafts for the foundation of bungalows. There is now, so far as I can ascertain, only one trading wherry left, and that is maintained by the Broadlands Wherry Trust and kept as a showpiece, a relic of a great past. She is called *Albion* and was for a time skippered by a scion of one of the most famous of the wherryman families, Nat Bircham. I went to school with Nat.

Yes, the Broads in my boyhood changed beyond all recognition. With their popularisation as a holiday venue, their old charm and haunting loveliness went. How did this happen? There is a story to it.

A worthy Norwich man, one John Loynes, a carpenter and joiner by trade, had visited the Broads and the river at Wroxham on fishing trips. He suddenly realised the immense possibilities of these natural beauty spots as a holiday attraction. Little could he have guessed what it was to lead to in the years that lay ahead. He trundled a boat on a handcart from Norwich, pushing it all the seven miles until he reached Wroxham Bridge. That journey must have been epic, since the road surface in those days was shocking. He established a small 'yacht station' on a marshy plot of ground on the Wroxham side of the bridge and set up business as the first hirer of yachts to holiday makers. He built no special boats – I am talking now of the turn of the century - but adapted fishing boats bought at Yarmouth and Lowestoft and made them suitable for hirers.

The Broads must have been paradise in the early days of the century, and demand for boats rapidly increased. Some of the boats he converted actually sailed as far as the inland waters of Holland, since the men who acted as skippers were in many cases seamen used to taking craft into deep water, but if I remember rightly, this side of his operations had disappeared by the time I was taking notice.

I can distinctly remember the yachts as they sailed upstream past our Caen Meadow. The boys and girls playing on the banks soon realised that the holiday people were a potential source of pocket money, and the sight of a yacht rounding the mill bend just below the Caen Meadow would cause great excitement among the youngsters. As the yacht approached, they would form themselves into a chanting choir singing a folk refrain which ran:

Old John Barleycorn
Old John Barleycorn
Give me a penny I'll sing you a song
Old John Barleycorn.

As the yacht slowly sailed along the river, the amused holidaymakers would throw coins from the boat into the water, and all and sundry would dive in to retrieve the treasure trove.

We from the schoolhouse were not permitted to join in this begging ploy, on pain of instant punishment and banishment from the Caen Meadow. We had to hold aloof, and I for one found it a very hard thing. Pocket money at the time was a halfpenny a week. To have to stand by and watch all this wealth being offered and not be permitted to partake was one of the hardest things ever. However, we bore no malice. Dadda and Mumma knew best and we bowed to their commands.

Just after the First World War the Broads as a playground became far more widely known, and the district began to be besieged by day trippers from Norwich, Yarmouth, Cromer and other holiday resorts of long standing in the neighbourhood. Rowing boats and skiffs were seen on the river in plenty. The distance down to the Broad at Wroxham by boat was beyond the prowess of all but the most muscular of oarsmen, as were the reaches of the river above the bridge. The local boatyard fraternity therefore turned its attention to cashing in on this obvious money-for-the-taking opportunity, and there began the first of the boats designed for the day tripper.

It was only rarely that we saw these boats at the end of the river, since they mostly catered for those who wanted to see the Broad, but quite a number would opt for the picturesque upper reaches of the Bure, and beautiful they were and are. One has only to turn the reach into Belaugh village and glimpse its venerable church presiding benignly over the scene, as it has done for long centuries, to be enraptured by the peace and tranquillity of the surrounds. Belaugh used to be one of the centres of wherry building, and in our day we would often see these wonderful craft lying alongside the jetty there, being repaired or perhaps breaking a journey so that the wherrymen could visit their families.

We had a joke in our district concerning Belaugh and its 'beach'. "Bin the Belaugh beach lately?" would be the opening gambit to ponderous jests about the peculiarities of the various Broadland villages. 'Belaugh Beach' was a small shelving strand where children could play safely in the mud and gravel. Possibly at some time, a spade and bucket and a sandcastle may have been seen there, causing local wit to fasten quickly on to 'Belaugh Beach' and the concept stuck, as has Wigan Pier further north. Now there is a staithe, a shop and a post office and water laid on, with other amenities for the yachting fraternity.

But I was talking of the day-trippers: the boats they used in the early days of the century were mostly steam powered. There was the *Blanche*, light blue, canopied and with a lovely swooping siren that used to delight us as the boat swung round the windmill corner with its cargo of trippers. The skipper would be warning us that 'Old John Barleycorn' would bring us a rich harvest. Then there was a steamer called the *Golden Arrow*. I have a vague recollection that it was varnished and had a midship's cabin where teas could be served, a polished brass funnel and a whistle. Legend has it that it belonged to the old Squire and that Jimmy Pitcher (old Jimmy), was its coxswain. I can't recall ever having seen it, but I think it met with disaster on one of its trips because we had a jingle we used to sing when one of its sister ships passed the Caen Meadow. It went to the tune of *We won't get home til the morning* and the jingle was no better nor worse than this:

The Golden Arrow got grounded
The Golden Arrow got grounded,
The Golden Arrow got grounded,
So hip hip hip hooray!

Unfeeling little brutes we were. Ambrose Thrower, a picturesque figure who had a yard by Wroxham Bridge opposite that of John Loynes, specialised in day boats. He had, I remember, two 'tin boats', as we called them. They were made of iron and were the first, and I should think the only, iron boats on our river. They were powered by such marine motors as there were in those days. He would actually let them to day trippers to look after themselves. I don't think they could have been very reliable, for many's the time I have seen one or other of them being towed home by Ambrose's pride, the steam launch Vivid. He loved that boat, and it was always his choice if he could persuade trippers to hire her in preference to the more sleek and aristocratic *King Edward*, Thames-built and very superior. She was motor-driven of course, with one of the noisiest marine engines I have ever heard - not noisy in the unpleasant sense but 'tinklingly' noisy, if you understand me. We could hear this curious tinkling noise long before she rounded the bend below the Caen Meadow reach. There were many other day boats; Loynes' yard had two very handsome launches, *Osprey* and *Blossom*, motor-driven and most genteel and comfortable. They were very popular, as was also *Aekoia*, a motor launch from the Horseshoes Hotel by Wroxham Bridge.

Memories come thick and fast of these boats, the first of the power boats to pollute the Broads. They were in their day very respectful to the sailing craft that they met in their travels. It is vastly different now, with powered boats of all kinds and sizes monopolising the waters and spoiling things for the genuine boat lover.

The history of the boatyards is a story of its own. One hopes it may be written before those of us who can remember it join our forebears in the quiet Broadland graveyards. Broadland as a national playground has arrived, but Broadland as a haven of beauty was not immediately surrendered to the foreigner. As I have remarked before, Mr Trafford, our local squire, who owned both sides of the river from Wroxham Bridge up to Belaugh, and possibly beyond, took steps with his poplar trees to preserve the river; at least he tried, and all praise to him for the attempt.

Here I am brought back again to the title of this book, since my four poplars were part of this protective policy. They were a sort of outpost of the forest, a last-ditch defence. They must have been the last of the poplars planted; possibly there were four saplings left over, and the men decided to plant them opposite the Bay to act as a kind of windbreak for us. Now they are gone, along with the squire who planted them and the hall where he lived. Other trees remain along the bank, but since most of the rivercraft today are motorboats, their obstructionist purpose has passed into oblivion.

In the evenings, those of us who know the tune of those trees and their rustling leaves can still hear them. They sing the old story of John Barleycorn, and the piping voices of the children who long ago sang that song is recorded in their music.

CHAPTER FOURTEEN

A unique village

"The past has revealed to me how the future is built"
Teilhard de Chardin, 1935

In the September 1971 issue of the *Norwich Churchman* there is a splendid photograph of the River Bure with the ruins of St Benet's Abbey in the background down near the mouth of the River Ant, one of the Bure's tributaries. The caption over the photograph reads as follows:

"St Benet's Abbey, where this year on the first Sunday in August, another annual service for holidaymakers was held. In the absence of the Bishop of Norwich, who is titular abbot of St Benet's, local clergy in the area decided that there should not be a break in the tradition and arranged a service themselves. The Rev. Wynter Blathwayt conducted the service and the Rev. Edward Everard, Vicar of Ranworth, preached. The service was attended by several hundred holidaymakers."

(I feel I should add here that there was, in the summer of 1971, an interregnum between Bishops, one having departed and another not expected until later in the year.)

My gaze fastened on the name Everard. When I was about 21, I and a companion, Jack Lawrence, had lunch with him in his vicarage at Ranworth. It must have been 1927. Here we are in 1971, and he is obviously still active. What memories both picture and caption brought to the fore.

Just after the Great War, we changed stationmasters in the village. A Mr Lawrence took over, bringing with him his family of wife and four children,

Margaret, Jack, Reggie and Bobby, with whom I became very friendly. I recalled my reunion with Margaret in the first chapter. The family moved into a house in Church Lane, just below the school and opposite to Haylett's Farm. The house was known as The Laundry, because some years previously it had served that purpose in the village.

There was a fine meadow behind the house, reaching down to the river. The meadow went with the house. It had its small staithe and boathouse within sight of the Bay on Caen Meadow, and of course my four poplars opposite. Mr Lawrence was very fond of the sport of coarse fishing, which was much indulged in on the Broads, so he had provided himself with a couple of row-boats.

He did a marvellous thing for his three sons, and indirectly I was fortunate enough to benefit from it. He bought the shell of a boat from an acquaintance of his who lived somewhere near Kings Lynn on the other side of the county, and had it brought by rail from Kings Lynn to Wroxham. It was transferred to a wagon, taken down to the meadow behind The Laundry and put into a shed which had been erected down by the river. Here it was to be made into a reasonably safe and watertight vessel and turned over to the Lawrence boys as their own boat.

Fred Pitcher, whom we met in the last chapter, was hired by Mr Lawrence to make the incomplete shell into a boat. On the principle of 'let your eye be your guide' Fred got to work on the boat. It was a flat-bottomed scow originally designed for the shallow waters of the Wash. Fred redesigned it so that there was a short covered-in deck in the bows, which had beneath it a capacious locker. The well of the boat was broken by three seats going athwartships, while the two after ones could be used as seats for rowing the craft and the shorter forward one took the hole for the mast to be stepped. Fred then made a slightly raised stern-sheets in the manner of a kind of quarter-deck. He fixed a shallow keel - about nine inches to a foot deep under the centre line of the flat bottom - and stepped a dinghy mast which would take a lug-sail and a jib.

It was a great day when the boat was launched, and Mrs Lawrence named her the *Query*. Jack was to be captain, Reggie First Mate and Bobby, the youngest boy, and I were deck-hands. The fun we had with that boat! If I could remember half of what went on, the history would fill volumes.

In the summer after the launch of the *Query*, we decided to set out on an expedition of exploration down the river. The burgee that we flew at the masthead had been designed and made by Margaret and was a white question mark on a blue background. I suppose I must have been about 16, Jack 13 and Reggie 11 or thereabouts. Bobby was only about seven or eight, and much to his annoyance was considered too young to come with us on this first venture. We set off on a Monday morning. Our sleeping quarters were on some wooden slatted floorboards taken from an old boat, which at night were laid across the two rowing seats. Golly, they were hard on the bones!

With the gaff of our sail and a pair of crutches made by Fred from some gash timber, and with a large square of canvas plus lacings, we were able to construct a reasonable awning for protection from the weather. We also took some of the rubberised groundsheets from the scouts' camping equipment to make doubly sure that we could be waterproof from above. We were very glad that we had done this as, when it did rain hard the drops were apt to come through our canvas awning, whose slope was a bit on the flattish side.

Our larder was magnificent. Mrs Lawrence saw to it by providing pre-cooked steak pies, a ham, sausage rolls and the like, so we certainly weren't going to die of starvation. There was a huge fruit cake, and buns and cookies too. For our own cooking facilities we had an old-fashioned twin burner 'Beatrice' oil stove. It fried our eggs and bacon and boiled the water for our tea, and was most effective. Mr Lawrence thought it a safer set-up than the Primus stoves used on yachts. Primuses could, in the hands of the awkward and impatient, blow up - never a yachting season passed without something of that sort happening. It was, of course, long before the days of Calor gas cookers.

The *Query* would only sail before the wind, or with a fairly strong wind on the port or starboard beam. Her lack of an adequate keel made sailing close to the wind or tacking an impossibility - she would slide sideways through the water like an old crab. So when the wind was not in our favour, I became Chief Engineer and managed our pair of heavy sweeps. Even so, we made very reasonable progress, and, following the customary use of the wherries, we would use both sweeps and sail together whenever possible. So we did fairly well, given our tackle.

Although I had lived in the Broads all my life, my knowledge of the river system covered only the area above Wroxham Bridge, that is, the waters in the immediate neighborhood of the school. Even so, just over the marshes from our Four Poplars there was an alder carr behind which hid two small broads known locally as Belaugh Broads, for the simple reason that they were in the village of Belaugh. They were a wonderful sanctuary and breeding ground for wild duck. We used to see them flighting over the Caen Meadow to alight on these broads. Apart from seeing these stretches of water from the top of Wroxham church tower, our awe of the Squire's preserves and the possible presence of his keepers kept us from approaching anywhere near those places.

Our voyage in the Query was therefore full of interest to all of us. We went by easy stages first to Wroxham Broad, where we enjoyed trying out her paces on that large stretch of water with plenty of wind. Then we tied up outside the main entrance to the Broad for the night. We didn't drop anchor on the Broad itself, as that carried a mooring charge and our meagre funds didn't run to such luxuries. On the following day we set off early and made for Ranworth, looking in on the Salhouse Broads en route. I had never visited Ranworth by water before and we were fascinated by the wonderful variety of water fowl. We also paid our first visit to Ranworth Church, and like all visitors, were much impressed with that famous Broadland shrine.

Nobody ever seems to have managed to state with any degree of exactitude how the Broads came into being, or at least I have never read any account which has satisfied me. Even old 'Sammy' Hewitt, our geography master when I was at City of Norwich School and who was pretty knowledgeable as I remember him at physical geography, didn't attempt to put forward a theory, although there the Broads lay before his very eyes. I think he just regarded them as a natural phenomenon created by the sluggish nature of the rivers winding through our flat countryside. Personally I was inclined to the theory that originally they were areas of marsh grasses, reeds and marsh plants and that, as in Ireland and Scotland, the local inhabitants with a scarcity of fuel for their fires dug peats. The Broads would therefore be old peat beds which filled with water from the rivers over the years. None of them are deep, and one can quite well accept the fact that peat digging some many years back accounts for some if not all of them. I know I will be shot down on this one but, after all, this is a book of memories and not a scientific treatise.*

We pushed on the next day for Potter Heigham on the Thurne, another tributary of the Bure. On the way, we tied up for an hour or so at the mouth of the Ant and walked the few yards of footpath to view the remains of St Benet's Abbey. We had to watch ourselves here, as the river began to feel the effect of the tide-flows at Yarmouth. When we turned into the Thurne we might have got into a lot of trouble in our clumsy craft if we hadn't taken account of the tide. Jack, as a good skipper, had been furnished with a book of tide tables by his father before we left home, so we were able to time our arrival at the mouth of the Thurne to coincide with slack water. Then we knew that we could catch the flood tide up to Potter Heigham with safety.

We really needed neither sweeps nor sail as the tide took us merrily to Potter Heigham. We met there a number of Wroxham yacht skippers whom we knew who called on us to inspect our craft. They had heard through the grapevine about Fred Pitcher's work on it, and most of them had never seen her and were anxious to give of their wisdom and quips. They weren't terribly impressed, as all, according to them, could have been done a lot better. But they admired our spunk in sailing her and congratulated Jack on his bringing her up with the tide. They enjoyed a cup of tea and a piece of cake

---

*It has indeed now been established that the Broads are a result of human activity. Excavations have shown that they are the result of rising sea levels flooding medieval peat excavations.

with us and accepted us into the fraternity of Broadland wanderers.

The novel-looking craft we were in caused a deal of comment from the owners of the more conventional yachts we met up with. I am writing, remember, of the very early 1920s. The ghastly power-cruiser with its attendant river-hog hadn't then polluted the Broads, and we respected their beauty and were, if I may put it thus snobbishly, gentlemen about it all.

On our way towards the Thurne, we met the Yarmouth pleasure steamer *Queen of the Broads* making one of her regular trips up to Wroxham Bridge. We got a salute from her siren, a cheer from the holidaymakers on board and a wave from the skipper – I believe his name was Captain Crisp, whom I knew.

I mustn't let a mention of *Queen of the Broads* pass without comment. She was part of the pattern of my early years in Wroxham. One would hear the unmistakeable hoot of her siren in the summer months, if the wind was in the right direction, as she made her turn into Wroxham Broad, and half an hour or so later as she arrived at Wroxham Bridge to disembark her passengers for lunch. Sometimes in the holidays it was possible to be down at the bridge to watch her arrival and her tying up at the Granary quay. It was a great thing actually to be on the quayside and to take the rope thrown by a deckhand and pass it through one of the ring bolts on the quay-heading. After the passengers disembarked and before the crew started on their own lunch, they would turn the long vessel round, using quants and lines, until she faced downstream ready for her return trip to Yarmouth in the afternoon.

I gather that the *Queen of the Broads'* up-river terminus is now at Horning, about ten miles downstream from Wroxham Bridge. What a pity! She is part of the history of Wroxham and it is sad to think that the bustle of her arrival and departure is gone and that no more will her friendly siren be heard in the reaches between Wroxham Broad and the bridge.

A well-known yachtsman of that day sighted us and came alongside to find out who we were and what we were sailing in. It was Mr H L Clarke from 'Down the Avenue' in Wroxham. He was sailing his superb black half-decker, on his way to a regatta. When he discovered who we were and what we were doing, he congratulated us on our turnout and wished us luck. It was all tremendous fun. On the trip we visited a number of riverside places and broads like Salhouse Little Broad, which we had never explored before. We even ventured up as far as South Walsham Broad, and that is no easy trip.

When we arrived back home at the end of the week we felt seasoned mariners. We had enjoyed ourselves enormously and felt we had really mastered the rivers and the Broads. I don't think I have ever done so much hard work in the rowing line as I did during that week. At the end of it I am sure that I would easily have got a place in an Oxford or Cambridge boat crew at the peak of their form. Query was no easy boat to row, particularly on the homeward run against the stream. But it was all great sport and I have always felt more than grateful to Mr and Mrs Lawrence for making such a marvellous trip possible and for their many kindnesses to me while they lived in Wroxham.

I remember writing my first attempt at a book on our return. I called it *The Cruise of the Query* and illustrated it with a map of our cruise, photographs we had taken en route and pen and ink sketches. I have often wondered what happened to that manuscript. A lot of hard work went into it. Perhaps it will turn up one day as a collector's piece. Who knows?

Anyway, to continue the saga of the *Query*, some years later at Whitsun Jack and I decided to go on a weekend cruise together. We picked on Ranworth as our target. Once again well victualled by our respective parents, we sailed, I think, on the Friday before Whit Sunday. This time, the wind being with us most of the way, we made Ranworth by evening and tied up at the public staithe on Ranworth Broad. We were very tired and after supper we were glad to get into our blankets with the prospect of a lazy rise on Saturday morning and a late breakfast.

There is a wonderful lullaby effect engendered by the chucklings, cluckings, quackings and whistlings made by waterfowl at night as they swim in and out of the reed beds going about their business. I can remember dropping off to sleep with this conversation to hand, wondering why the stupid creatures didn't do likewise. There were coots and water-hens (moorhens), dabchicks and ducks of various species. One woke in the morning to find the same discussion still going on. I have come to the conclusion that waterfowl are among the biggest gossips in the whole of nature.

After breakfast we sauntered up to the village, where we found notices advertising a concert to be held in the village hall that evening. We wandered up to find where the hall was and there found the vicar, who hadn't long been in the parish, looking very fussed. He said a sort of absent-minded good morning to us and asked whether or not we were visitors. "Yes and no" we replied, and introduced ourselves. His name was Everard – yes, the same Mr Everard with whom I started off this chapter. He was delighted to discover that we had nothing better to do than offer to help. Immediately we were set to work putting out chairs, hanging curtains and doing a thousand and one odd jobs.

In order to keep tabs on us and make sure he would have our assistance in the afternoon, he invited us to lunch. We had a fantastic lunch, consisting of soup, cold ham and salad, apple pie and cheese and lashings of lemonade, together with the most amusing flow of conversation from our host, who was getting the proceeds of the concert as a donation towards the restoration fund he was setting up for his church.

After lunch we went back to the hall to complete our work. The son of the local big landowner, a Mr Cater, was in charge of the concert, and we were rapidly signed on by him as a back-stage party for the evening. We thoroughly enjoyed ourselves. The concert was like most village concerts, a mixture of good and mediocre, but for me there was one outstanding artist, a baritone who sang familiar ballads very well indeed. I remember that during the last of his numbers he sang two songs I have never heard sung since that night. Each had a refrain that has lasted in my musical memory. I would dearly love to know where I can find them. The first had a refrain that went:

'Slow, slow you great black crow.
There's nothing so slow as a great black crow!'

And the other:

'I saw Esau sitting on a seesaw.
I saw Esau kissing Kate.
The fact is we all three saw;
For I saw Esau, he saw me
And she saw I saw Esau.'

I have only ever heard them that once.

I have always remembered with the warmest of feelings that delightful Whitsun Weekend at Ranworth. Jack and I often talked of it after. I can remember so clearly before dropping off to sleep in the old Query hearing the chattering of the innumerable flocks of wildfowl. Both Jack and I enjoyed every moment of our stay and left to return home to Wroxham on the Tuesday after with feelings of real regret.

It is strange how coincidence seems to take charge throughout one's life. On August 30 1971, the day I was writing my memories of Ranworth on that Whitsun weekend, my attention was drawn to the following obituary notice in the London Daily Telegraph:

"The Rev. Edward Everard, Vicar of Ranworth, Norfolk since 1926 and known as "The Bishop of the Broads" died at the weekend aged 80. His church of St Helen's is often described as the "Cathedral of the Broads" because of the services he holds for Broads visitors. While he was at Ranworth more than £15,000 was spent on restoring the Church. Most of the money was given by holidaymakers."

I count myself fortunate to have met and known him and feel it a great privilege, even so many years ago, that Jack and I were permitted, in our small way, to have helped raise that £15,000. May his gallant soul rest in peace.

It was about this time that Dadda retired after 33 years as headmaster of the village school. They marked his retirement with a presentation and with tokens of great affection and love from all the village, from the children and their parents and from the many who had passed through Dadda's hands, some of them now had children of their own in Dadda's care. It was a very moving occasion.

With part of the 'lump sum' that he received from the State on his retirement, he bought a small motor-boat. I'm afraid that we youngsters had far more use out of that boat than did Dadda and Mumma. It opened up the Broads to me in a way that I had never known before, and there were few places on the Bure that we did not visit. I had a bosom pal then called Fred Buck, whose nickname was Peter. Peter and I covered as many of the Broads and rivers as we could.

I also bought my own first boat at that time. It was a tatty old gun-punt, and I bought it for a pound as it lay. It had been half-sunk in a dyke for some time and, in consequence, was in a very bad state of repair. Peter and I dragged it out of the water and patched it up as best we could. We never succeeded in making it absolutely waterproof, but it got us around. My brother-in-law, Algie Filby, who was a boat builder, was quite horrified with its state and flatly refused to have anything to do with it. However Peter and I fixed it up with a small mast and sail, which was very useful at times, but mostly we paddled it, one of us forward and the other aft in the manner of canoeists.

We decided on a local exploration of the waterways around us. The gun-punt was very shallow drafted and would edge along dykes and backwaters with ease and without any danger of running aground. It was also very low in the water, as all gun-punts are. They are built in that fashion to enable the wildfowler to creep up in the shelter of the reeds to the duck or other waterfowl he wishes to shoot. Peter and I did no shooting of waterfowl. For one thing we had no gun and for the other, even if we had, we wouldn't have used it to kill birds. We were much too interested in watching them and in spotting new species we hadn't seen before.

What we most liked doing was to go down to Wroxham Broad in the motor-boat towing the gun-punt astern of us. We would leave the motor-boat hidden from vulgar gaze in a hide-out we had discovered on the edge of the Broad and then take the punt and set off on our voyages of exploration down the many dykes that criss-crossed through the marshes and alder carrs on the Wroxham bank of the Broad. It was a great thrill if we approached a bungalow where the dyke or cut went underneath, the bungalow itself being built on piles. We would hear people talking above our heads as we made our stealthy way under their floor and through to the further side.

I haven't been down that way for more years than I care to count, but I should imagine that most of the waterways that we explored in the glorious summers of the middle and late twenties are now silted up and impassable. I'd dearly love to have a look round and see whether they are still in being.

One other chancy expedition that we embarked on was to leave Wroxham Broad and go out into the river and then make for the 'cut' which led to Hoveton Broad, at that time private water and forbidden to the general public. We discovered that by artful and careful manipulation, if the river wasn't running too high, we could get ourselves and the punt under the chained and padlocked five-barred gate which barred the approaches of the broad to ordinary craft. Here we had to watch ourselves. It wouldn't do to be discovered on those waters, so we had to go discreetly and warily lest we came unawares on some authorised angler fishing the waters for pike or perch. Over the seasons we did manage to explore most of the edges of that broad, always with our hearts in our mouths lest we should be caught.

Once we essayed an assault on Belaugh Broads. Opposite the staithe of the Priest's House in Wroxham there is a long cut flanked by an avenue of tall poplars. At the end of this cut there is the inevitable five-barred gate with chains and padlock. The old Squire had put it there to keep out people like Peter and me, but it didn't matter what the state of the river, we never managed to pass that portal and I have never been on Belaugh Broad.

Stanley Stevenson told me a short while ago that he remembered going up there once with his father and a friend. They had asked for and had been given permission by the Squire to do some pike fishing there. They had rowed up the river from the Caen Meadow and met Mr Hagan, the Squire's head gamekeeper, waiting on the Priest's staithe. He handed over the key to the gate, which was attached, said Stanley, to "the biggest wooden tally you'd ever seen, so that if you dropped it in the drink it wouldn't sink." Apparently they had a wonderful day's sport, as the pike were unused to the wiles of fishermen and fell easy prey to their skill. They got some whoppers, so Stanley told me.

But to return for a short while to Wroxham Broad. I remarked that Peter and I found a hide-out on the Broad as a base for our expeditions. It was an old deserted summerhouse and boat house, painted green. I think it must have belonged to Wroxham House at one time and had been forgotten when the house had changed hands at some time or another. In our day it was neglected and unused, but the last occupants had left some old cane lounge chairs in the room above the boathouse, together with a small table. Peter and I made that our base for our many expeditions. We cached a kettle, a frying pan and some tin mugs there, and kept tea and tinned milk. All these things we hid very carefully in a sort of loft, so that any *bona fide* visitor to the place, gardener, gamekeeper or even the owner, wouldn't know we had taken possession. During the long summer holidays we would decide on a long afternoon and evening down there, leave the motor-boat hidden in the boathouse and taking the punt on one of our trips down the cuts and backwaters, returning to the summerhouse for a meal in the evening before setting off back home by river.

If we happened to come across a coot's or water-hen's nest with a fair clutch of eggs, we would remove one or two and scramble them in our frying pan over an open fire in the woods. We found what might almost be described as a little island of firm ground in the marshes close by the summerhouse, and there we would light our fire and have our picnic. We were always most careful to put the fire out and destroy any evidence of our having been there. We never took anybody else with us or let on to anybody what we doing or where we were doing it, and made quite sure that we wouldn't be followed. This place and all our explorations concerned with it was peculiar to ourselves, a sort of bridge between boyhood and manhood, and it was a very, very happy time.

One other expedition we made at this time is worthy of note. One of our school acquaintances, a chap called Leslie Bunting, invited us both to spend the inside of a week with him at a beach hut owned by his parents at a place called Sea Palling, the nearest sea beach to Wroxham, some 10 to 12 miles. We looked at the map – we had been there by road – and Peter and I decided to go to Palling by water. Leslie was going down with his parents for the weekend before our visit and they would be returning to Wroxham on the Monday morning. We had to take blankets and so on and some food. Having gathered all our impedimenta, we loaded up the motor-boat and off we set, with a spare two-gallon tin of petrol in case of emergencies. To reach the nearest point to Sea Palling on the Broad's waterways involved quite a considerable journey and, at the point of arrival, some risk about the depth of water for the motor-boat, to say nothing of the hazard of water weeds round the propeller.

We set out on the Monday for Waxham Creek, the nearest navigable point to Sea Palling. Our trip involved going down the Bure as far as the mouth of the Thurne, then up through Potter Heigham Bridge and across Horsey Mere. We then had to find a badly-marked dyke to take us up to Waxham. We called at Horsey village to get directions and were told we would be taking a risk because of the depth of water.

Fortune favoured us. There was enough water in the dyke, and we arrived safely at our destination at Waxham. We then had to hump our kit across the marshes, with the sand dunes of the coast in sight all the way. We eventually made the beach hut to find Leslie awaiting us. We had a glorious week there with wonderful weather, good swimming in the sea and a thoroughly lazy existence for the week, regretfully returning, with no further mishap, to Wroxham on the Saturday. It was a most wonderful end to a wonderful summer and also, one might add here, a most satisfactory and delightful finale to a very, very happy boyhood.

CHAPTER FOURTEEN

At the end of that summer I left home for the first time, to go to the old St Mark and St John College in Battersea to be trained as a schoolmaster. It was the end of one era and the dawn of another; the end of my childhood.

After that Wroxham became a place to be visited instead of the place where I lived, but the memories of those 18 happy years remain with me as the most important years of my life. No boy could ever have had so happy a home in such marvellous surroundings, with such loving guidance and so many good and worthy friends.

Truly, it was unique.

ND - #0489 - 270225 - C0 - 234/156/18 - PB - 9781908223227 - Matt Lamination